Removing Your Mask

No More Hiding From Your Truth

Marion Moss

Orion Publishing Company
Seattle, Washington

Removing Your Mask,
No More Hiding From Your Truth
Copyright © 1992 by Marion Moss.

Cover Design Copyright © 1992 by Jennifer Law
Edited by Rosemary Warden
Back cover photo by Scott Hubbard

Library of Congress Cataloging in Publication Data

Moss, Marion   1954-
    Removing your mask : no more hiding from your
    truth / Marion Moss
    p.   cm.
    Includes bibliographical references and index.
    ISBN 0-9631341-0-8 (pbk.) : $13.95
    1. Self-acceptance. 2. Self-actualization   (Psychology)
3. Self-respect. I. Title.
BF575.S37M67 1992
158'.1--dc20   91-43892
                                 CIP

Published by:
Orion Publishing Company
539 Queen Anne Avenue, Suite 156
Seattle, WA   98109
(206) 633-5742

Printed in the United States of America.

Printed with soy-based ink and on recycled paper because we care about the planet.

*To **Richard**,
my partner, whose love and support
continues to urge me
to live from my truth*

Contents

Part 2
The Lies of the Mask

Part 3
Shedding the Layers of the Mask

Acknowledgments

Writing this book has been a significant piece of my process of self-discovery. There are many people who have inspired, nudged, supported, and challenged me to remove *MY MASK* and live from my truth. Those mentioned here are by no means the only ones who have helped bring me to this point. I feel that everyone who has been in my life has played an important part. I thank you all!

The following people hold a special place in my heart. They have given me gifts at key moments in my growth when I have most needed them:

Richard Hubbard, my partner, to whom this book is dedicated. He nurtures me in ways I never believed were possible. He is helping me to trust again and know that I am always supported. He makes it safe to be vulnerable and encourages me to live my life's purpose.

Holly Bell, my lifelong dearest friend. She loves me no matter what or how far apart we live. She reminds me of what I already know when I temporarily forget.

Anne Grothaus-King, my close friend and fellow seeker of truth. She helps me to spiritually spiral upward by loving me just how I am. She gives me a haven to explore my truth.

Elaine Dines, my dear friend and "Shen" energy healer. She is a walking angel of love. She helps me to understand this life is a journey of the heart. She affirms for me that it is possible to be both strong and gentle.

Susan Ellis, my friend and former therapist. She has given me the best gift any therapist can possibly give–she has shown me how to be my own therapist.

Ed Hess, my friend and colleague. He lives the life of a facilitator and true leader. He strives to bring the ways of truth into the real world.

Introduction

Several years ago, I began writing a journal specifically to explore my fear issues. Fear seemed to be an underlying theme of my life, even though I believed that I presented a strong exterior. As I wrote, an image for my feelings became clear. The scene was a haunted house. I was creeping around every corner waiting for something to jump out and frighten me. I put on my "brave mask," walking with authority and whistling a happy tune. But underneath I was terrified and wondered if my false bravery would fool anyone.

This was a metaphor for my life. I attempted to show a "together" mask to the world. But fear was an undercurrent which undermined my effort to obtain lasting happiness. I hated to admit that I had so much fear because I wanted to believe the illusion of being so together. I wanted to believe that I could really be what my mask said that I was. I wanted to show myself that I was tough and could handle anything. And I wanted to cover the deep emptiness I felt.

Through the haunted house image, I realized that I had to decide whether I was willing to continue living in fear behind a false mask, or whether I chose to walk freely in the world, unafraid. Part of me doubted that I could live authentically without a mask. But something inside said I could. In an act of faith, I decided to choose freedom.

In so choosing, I didn't realize how much inner examination and understanding lay ahead before I would feel safe enough to shed the mask, layer by layer. I didn't know how raw I would feel by exposing my bare face to the world. I didn't understand how to end the fear beneath the disguise of the mask. And I didn't anticipate the lightness, joy and inner peace I would experience through letting it go.

I am now beginning to live with more lightness, joy and inner peace. I have made discoveries about myself and others which were impossible to make while all those layers of the mask weighed me down. As I peel away the false coverings, I feel freer to experience life fully and to get on with what I want to do.

What I present to you is a synthesis of my truth and the inner process which has gotten me to this point. I do not pretend that I am able to live consistently from it. I continue to grow and learn ways to remove even more layers of my mask to which I cling. This book is my reminder of what must be *lived*, not just talked about.

There are many ways through which people can approach their healing process and realize their dreams. But there is no simple formula which will fix everyone. Tender feelings must be acknowledged and accepted for what they are. And everyone's process is valid for them, no matter what it looks like on the outside to others. What I present is given out of love. It is intended to act as a catalyst in supporting you to *reach within yourself for your own answers*. I hope that you will keep the pieces of my experience and truth which fit for you and feel free to throw out the rest. After all, that is what we each must do if we are to remove our masks and become our true selves.

Marion Moss
Seattle, Washington
December 1991

Part 1
Hiding Behind the Mask

CHAPTER 1
The Mask Revealed

"Mask—A covering for the face or part of the face, to conceal or disguise the identity."
Webster's New World Dictionary

Imagine that you have been invited to a costume party. You are very excited about going. You like costume parties because it is fun to play the role of someone else. It sends you back to your childhood joy of playing make believe. You get to choose the person you want to be.

You prepare for the party with great enthusiasm. You design a mask you feel best fits your character. You think about how you will present yourself at the party to play the part. You practice around the house being that person. You mimic the speech, movements, and demeanor of your chosen role.

When you get to the party, your world of make believe transforms you into your character. You *are* that person for the evening. You whirl around the dance floor, dazzle your date, and make your friends gasp in awe at the expertise with which you play the role. The evening is a fairy tale come true.

Then the party is over and you go home. But you have had so much fun that you hate to take off the mask. You loathe going back to being who you really are. You don't like being yourself. You want to hold onto the magic of the evening as long as possible so you decide to wear the mask to bed.

The next morning you get up and go into the bathroom. You forget that you are still wearing the mask as you absentmindedly begin to brush your teeth. When you try to put the toothbrush into your mouth, you hit the mask instead. You look in the mirror with shock as you see that there is someone other than you staring back. You try to take the mask off but you find that removing it is not as easy as you thought. It is stuck to your face because it has been on so long. With panic and horror, you try to rip off the mask, only to find that it is firmly affixed to your skin. Now what are you going to do? You can't live with the mask on, but you don't know how you can get your real face back.

Luckily this situation is only a metaphor. Masks can be fun to wear occasionally, when we know that we are pretending. But when we become attached to them, and want to deny the existence of the real person underneath, we begin to feel smothered by the very thing which at first felt so good.

What Is the Mask?

We all wear masks from time to time to hide our real selves. As the dictionary states, a mask conceals our true identity. It shields who we actually are. It protects our real selves from a perceived outside threat. A mask is the cover we present to the world to tell others about ourselves. It conveys a message, "I want you to see me *this* way."

HIDING BEHIND THE MASK

If, however, we wear a mask while having forgotten that we are pretending, we can start to cause ourselves damage. It is as if the true self is knocking on the mask from the inside, screaming, "Hey, you out there. Let me out. Remember me? I can't breathe." We know we are uncomfortable but we are unaware that it is the mask that is causing the discomfort. We have confused the mask with the true self.

In an effort to conform to the shape of the mask, we begin to behave in ways that don't fit our internal truth. Our energy is tied up in dealing with the mask. The more we focus our attention away from our truth, the more we feel uncomfortable about facing others without the mask. We can't remember what our truth is or who we are. It is important for us to realize that the *behavior* we have when wearing the mask is *not the real us*. It is a sham, a pretense used to prevent the true self from being exposed and hurt.

As we become more aware that we are wearing a mask, we begin to want to shed it. However, we have mixed emotions about how to deal with the mask. We sometimes want to rip it off quickly to get rid of it. But when we try to do that, we feel too raw and unprotected. At other times we prefer to cling to the mask for security and familiarity. But this makes us feel weak and as if we are living a lie.

This book is about finding ways to remove the mask without damaging ourselves. It is about discovering and honoring our truth beneath the mask. It is about seeing other people as they truly are and learning how to love them and express our truth to them. It is also about *living without the mask in the pure joy of being ourselves!* Removing the mask will help us eliminate the artificial barriers which separate us from ourselves, others, and the world around us.

Why Did We Agree to Wear Masks?

"I like your mask. Did you make it yourself?"

We didn't know the rules of the game when we agreed to wear masks. We were children, simple and curious about life. We were like sponges, soaking up experiences, observing the world around us, and learning how to be people.

At first, wearing masks was like a game of peek-a-boo. It made us laugh and it made our parents happy so we agreed to wear them. We didn't know that adults were serious about the "game of mask."

Then one day we started to take off the masks and we got punished or ignored. We didn't want to wear them, but we wanted to be loved and noticed so we kept them on. Adults seemed to like us better with our masks on. They responded to us. They proudly showed us, in our masks, to their friends. And we were rewarded for wearing them. We began to think that we could only be loved if we wore masks.

Then we went to school. We arrived our first day with shiny shoes and new clothes. We also had our masks which were becoming very finely decorated by now with ornate patterns and glitter. Our teachers looked at our masks approvingly and may even have told our parents what a fine job they had done of helping to design our masks. When the teachers weren't looking and we were with other children, we decided to take off our masks. We felt the cool air on our faces and could breathe again. It made us feel happy and alive. Then the teachers saw us and scolded us. They made it clear that it was not polite to show our bare faces. They sent notes home to our parents telling them that we had exposed our faces in class. After a while, some of us gave up and decided to wear the masks given or self-created, in order to avoid more trouble or hurt.

Some children decided that they didn't like their masks so they smashed them into the ground. They were punished severely by the adults for having naked faces. The children who kept their masks, ridiculed and pummelled them until their faces were bloodied and bruised. Reluctantly, the rebels made new masks for themselves out of very hard material which could not be penetrated by the stings and barbs of others. They knew it was much safer to wear a thick, protective covering than to reveal themselves.

There are very few adults who do not wear masks. Most of us have been influenced by the circumstances, events, and people in our lives. Although we are not always aware of these influences, they can impact how we feel and the face we show to others. It is important to recognize that, as adults, we have a choice. No one can make us wear masks any longer. It is up to us to decide if we are willing to risk taking them off or if we choose to keep our true selves hidden behind facades, screaming to be let out.

CHAPTER 2
Games of the Mask

"Oh boy, a game! Can I play too?"

Why We Play the Games

We know why we began playing the "games of the mask" as children. We had to for our survival. We did it to get the sustenance, love, and nurturing that were needed to survive. But why do we continue to play the "games of the mask" now, as adults? Why don't we choose something different?

Part of the reason is that most of us are unaware that we are playing games. We are so embroiled in the games themselves that we don't have the energy or understanding to step back and see ourselves as players.

Some of us see the games and are frustrated at being sucked into them. But we don't know how to extract ourselves. We are tired of hiding from our truth. Yet we receive only periodic glimpses of what that truth is. The times of insight are so infrequent that we may feel as if they are illusions, the unrealistic or unattainable fantasies.

Another factor which keeps most of us from ending the game playing is fear of the unknown. We may yearn for bliss, but fear that the unknown will hold death or pain instead. So, reluctantly we settle for a constant dull pain rather than risk stepping outside of the familiar games.

Whatever our reasons, we can choose to avoid assuming the *adult* responsibility required to quit playing the games. We can remain mental, emotional, and spiritual children. We can continue to blame others, the system, society, or anyone who serves as scapegoat for our problems. Through the games, everybody can be at fault, except our own masks.

Rules of the Games

All of the games can be played with one or more players. All 5.5 billion humans (or however many are currently inhabit this planet) can participate.

None of the "games of the mask" require experience to play. There are no playbooks to study before you enter a particular game. You can get into the games at any point, no matter how long they have already been played by others before you.

No special equipment needs to be purchased prior to joining the games. The only thing you need is your mind. (The more experienced players will shape your mind in the manner necessary for playing a particular "game of the mask.")

Selecting a Part to Play in the Games

It will be necessary for you to play a role in all of the "games of the mask." You may want to begin thinking about the role you prefer (or are already playing).

It is okay for you to duplicate someone else's role. In fact, that can make for a more exciting game. You can also switch parts in mid-game. Be forewarned that to do this will cause very interesting dynamics which you should be prepared to handle.

In the next chapter, we will take a look at some of popular masks, but first we'll examine the games that are played.

The Game of "Bully/Victim"

Players

You will need at least two people to play this game, but there can be an infinite number of players. At least one person acts as a bully and one person acts as a victim. (*Note*: This game can be played solitaire if the person is willing to play the roles of both the bully and the victim.)

Object of the Game

Denial of everyone's truth by use of intimidation and fear.

Rules of the Game

1. Bullies:
   a. Act superior and in control.
   b. Must not let down their guard or open their hearts. (This would be a serious rule violation.)
2. Victims:
   a. Act worthless and out of control.
   b. Must not show their strength.

3. Bullies always feel superior to the victims. If there is more than one bully, one becomes the "top bully" (unless there is a deal made to carve up territories).
4. Conflict and strife are required. The more turmoil the better. Bonus chips will be given for outstanding examples of strife between players. (Collection of chips will be discussed later.)
5. None of the players can let the others see their truth or the real person underneath. To do so will cause the following consequences:
   a. *First time rule violation.* The other players can ridicule and ostracize to keep the truth from being told again.
   b. *Second time rule violation.* The player can be ganged up on by all other players and pummelled physically, verbally, and spiritually to let the violator know that the situation will not be tolerated.
   c. *Subsequent rule violations.* If the player violating the rules is still functioning, the other players can put this person into the special "bully's circle." The violator will have to wear the "bully's target" on his/her back for the rest of the game. Any time a game player feels like it, he/she can abuse the violator in any manner which feels appropriate. There is no way to escape the "bully's circle," unless the other players vote that good behavior has been demonstrated long enough to create confidence that no other violation will occur.

How the Moves Are Made

Bullies go around the room stomping, screaming, and making cutting verbal remarks. They can abuse others, especially those who are smaller, younger, or weaker than they are. It is helpful to find others' flaws and pick on them. It is also appropriate for the bullies to carry weapons (or pretend to have them), and to hit people whenever they want.

Bullies can take a more subtle approach if they choose. They can give the "You're dead if you even think it" look, the stare, the raised eyebrow, or the pointed finger. Flared nostrils, clenched jaws, and tapping feet will give them bonus chips, if they are able to get their victims to stop in their tracks.

If victims try to point out what bullies are doing to them, bullies should deny any responsibility for what they have done. They should turn the responsibility back on the victim with statements like, "You provoked me." "You have a problem with that?" "What's wrong with you?" "I never said that to you." "Read my lips!" "What are you trying to get away with?" or "What's your problem?"

Victims go around the room wringing their hands, worrying, apologizing, or acting scared, stupid, numb, or trapped. They can nervously clean house, get involved in other people's lives, and play "ain't it awful" with friends.

It is a good idea for victims to stoop their shoulders, hang their heads, and shuffle. It helps if victims do not look directly into the eyes of the bullies. This will not be considered staying in character and chips will be taken away.

Victims can get bonus chips by being especially nice to the ones bullying them. After the bully has done something particularly mean, bonus chips will be given for saying such things as, "I'm sorry I provoked you. It won't happen again." "I deserved that." "Please do it to me again, if I get out of line." "I didn't mean to offend you." or "I'll be more careful next time."

Accumulating Chips

Chips are accumulated by outstanding examples of playing in character. Both bullies and victims can accumulate chips. Only the bullies determine who receives how many chips for certain performances. The more dramatic the performance, the better. The following criteria will be used for obtaining chips:

1. Conflict and strife - The longer, more complicated, exceptional situations will be awarded extra bonus chips.
2. Intimidation of victims in a particularly short time.
3. Bullies who are able to make victims grovel for more than 5 seconds without getting up.
4. Bullies who can manipulate and control multiple victims.

5. Bullies who can say the most outrageous statement to a victim and are believed.
6. Victims who live in constant fear that they will be hurt.
7. Victims who grovel at the feet of bullies for long periods of time.
8. Victims who will not question anything that is told to them by bullies (e.g., "Jump off a cliff").
9. Victims who are so completely cowed that even pets can bully them.

Deducting Chips

Chips can also be taken away. This, too, occurs at the discretion of the bullies. The following criteria will be used for taking away chips:
1. Anyone telling the truth. The only situation requiring an automatic loss of at least one chip.
2. Bullies who open their hearts.
3. Victims who show strength.
4. Anyone trying to resolve conflict and strife by means other than bullying or playing victim.

Determining the Winner

Players who are still alive at the end of the game and have accumulated the most chips will be the winners. There can be multiple winners in the first round. But they will be obligated to play another round, to determine a "sudden death play-off" winner.

The Game of "Let's Pretend"

Players

Any number of people can play this game. It is well-suited for playing in families with drug, alcohol, or codependency issues. It is also a good solitaire game.

Object of the Game

Denial of the truth by pretending that the obvious is not present.

Rules of the Game

1. No one is to speak the truth or see the repeated patterns of themselves or others.
2. Keeping secrets is a must. Chips will be taken away if any secrets are disclosed (especially to anyone not playing the game).

How the Moves Are Made

One person is assigned the role of a rhinoceros which stands anywhere it wants. This player is to be ignored even if it breaks windows or emits loud, obnoxious sounds.

Everyone else goes around the rhinoceros, pretending that it is not there. In fact, it might be best for someone to throw a tablecloth over the rhino while the other players are not looking, so it will be easier to ignore. (*Note*: If a player is seen putting a tablecloth over the rhinoceros, the other players are to act as if the whole incident did not occur.)

Accumulating Chips

The player who is most oblivious to the truth, will be the person who gives out the chips. Chips are accumulated by everyone keeping their mouth shut about the truth. Periodically, players can be given extra chips just to show appreciation for the fact that the truth has not been exposed.

Deducting Chips

1. Chips are taken away for:
   a. Noticing the rhinoceros
   b. Drawing attention to its existence
2. Telling the truth or revealing *any* game secrets to other players or to anyone outside the game.

Determining the Winner

All players are winners as long as no one speaks the truth or says the obvious.

If players have chips deducted for violations of the rules, they can be declared losers or scapegoats. The game continues, but if anything goes wrong, the scapegoat can be blamed.

Variations of the Game

Many game variations can be played. Here are some of the most common:

Game of "Pretend You Don't Know Yourself"

This game is best played solitaire, but can be played with other people. The object is to act as if you don't know who you are. You play the role of someone whom you think others want you to be. You get chips for saying things like, "Oh, I'm too dumb to figure that out." "I just don't know what has come over me." or "I don't know what made me say such a thing."

Game of "Pretend You Don't Know You Are Hurting Yourself"

This is best played in a family setting or with friends. The object is to make others think that you don't know that you are hurting yourself. You play the masochist role. You get chips for doing things like cutting your wrists, banging your head on the wall, having repeated accidents, or sitting in a dark room listening to depressing music. If anyone confronts you about why you were hurting yourself, you say, "I didn't know I was hurting myself." or "That didn't hurt."

Game of "Pretend You Are Bad"

This can be played with any number of people and any setting, but is especially good to play if you are a child or are in an intimate relationship. The object is to convince yourself and others that you are a bad person, rotten to the core.

You play the role of the troublemaker or saboteur. If you are a child, you get chips for doing such things as poisoning the neighbor's dog, throwing rocks at cars, picking fights, or stealing things.

As a partner you get chips for having affairs, forgetting birthdays, or always being late. If there is more than one "bad" player, you should find out who is the "baddest" of them all. That person gets bonus chips.

Game of "Pretend You are Confused"
This can be played in a group of people, but it is best played one-on-one or as solitaire. The object is to convince yourself or others that you are confused about your truth. You may play the role of the absentminded-but-lovable person. You get chips for statements like, "I don't know. My brain is just all mixed up." "I just can't think straight." or "I haven't got a clue."

Other Games of the Mask

Game of Hide and Seek

This game is played best in a work setting or in a love relationship. The object is for you to hide from other people and give them just enough of a clue about your truth that they are intrigued and will try to seek out the real you. You play the role of mouse in this cat-and-mouse game. You want to leave enough of a trail that they will want to look for you, but you never let them get close enough to know the real you or your truth. In love relationships, this game can go on for years. While you may never let anyone close enough to you to get the love you want, you will never get badly hurt either. The pursuit itself substitutes for the love. Your energy is so tied up in the hide-and-seek that you can forget that you are keeping yourself from being deeply loved or known for who you really are.

Quick-Change Mask

This game can be played with many players. The object is to have as many different masks as possible so that no one knows the real you. Everyone will see just a piece of the truth without having enough pieces to know your true self. The roles you play will differ with each person you are with. You may have so many roles that your energy will be consumed in keeping the roles straight. After a while you may forget who you really are because your focus has been on the roles rather than on yourself. That's okay. Just pick a role you've played and convince yourself you are that person. It has fooled other people, maybe you can fool yourself.

Game of Nonresponsibility

This game is played by as many people as are willing to play. It is similar to the game of "toss," except a "hot potato of responsibility" is used. The object is to get rid of the "hot potato of responsibility" as quickly as possible by tossing it to someone else. The potato cannot touch the ground, however. It must always be in someone's hands or in the air.

If the potato comes to you, you must start blaming someone else and saying it is not your fault. If you are able to get the person you blamed hooked into responding to your accusation, then you can toss the potato to them. You get bonus chips for coming up with creative excuses why you are not responsible. Extra chips will be given to those players who are able to blame the most other people by the end of the game.

Game of Struggle

This game is best played in pairs or solitaire, although entire groups can play. The object is to decide that you want something, but sabotage yourself from getting it. In this game the players all play the role of the mythological character, Sisyphus. (Sisyphus was doomed to roll a stone uphill, only to have the stone fall to the bottom. Then he would have to start over again. He did this for an eternity.) In the "Game of Struggle" each player will get to choose what their own stone will represent. Some examples of struggle are: "I'll never get to have any fun." "Life's a bitch, and then you die." "Nobody will ever love me." "Anything worth having must be worked for." and "No pain, no gain."

After players have selected their "stone of struggle", they start rolling their stones looking longingly off in the distance at the mirage of the goal they think they want. (*An important note*: The stone must always be kept between the player and the goal.) The goal can never quite be reached. Anyone who does, loses all chips and is declared an instant loser.

CHAPTER 3
Wearing Our Favorite Masks

"Mirror, Mirror, on the Wall.
Who's the Masked One at this Ball?"

To play the "games of the mask", you must select masks to wear. You can choose from ones mentioned here, or you can create your own.

Emotional Masks

If you choose to wear an emotional mask, you will play at being emotionally out of control. Emotions must override judgment and common sense. You will need to be so into your own perceptions of the world that you do not see any way of being other than your own. Behind the emotions is a desperate plea for love, because you feel unlovable.

Tasmanian Devil

As the Tasmanian Devil, you unload emotionally on whoever or whatever is in your path. You are like a tornado sucking up everything as it rips through a trailer park. Since you have no clear internal sense of what you really feel, your emotions are chaotic. You may be crying and screaming in one instant, throwing things, *and* feeling immense grief. You have no sense of others' existence when you are in the middle of whirling through a room.

Your emotional energy is spent very quickly, though, because it came out in such a fury. The storm of emotions passes and you see the devastation you've caused. You feel guilty, but don't know how to keep the outbursts from returning again.

Puddle on the Floor

As the Puddle on the Floor, you collapse in an emotional puddle whenever there is pressure on you, you have to make a decision, or you are challenged in any way.

Your collapse can take many forms. You can get too sick to leave your bed. You can get so severely depressed that all you do is sit at home, read romance novels, and eat. Or you can be so numb that you leave for several days without telling others where you are. Whatever the form, you are unable to function in your day-to-day tasks and are emotionally overwhelmed.

Hysterical Hyena

As Hysterical Hyena, you shriek your emotions at the top of your lungs no matter where you are or who you are with. You do not notice or care if you disturb others' peace of mind. Your need to draw attention to yourself is so great that you start out at the highest possible volume. After awhile, though, people ignore you because you are like the little boy who cried wolf one too many times. No one believes that your pleas for attention are serious. The very attention you so desperately want eludes you because you are so irritating to be around.

Angry Masks

If you choose to wear an angry mask, you will try to "unload" your anger on others. There may be a temporary sense of relief, but then you feel badly at a deep level that you have dumped on others and are unable to deal with your anger in another way.

Bully in a China Shop

As the Bully in a China Shop, you are like the Merrill Lynch bull wreaking havoc on all of the fragile merchandise in a fine china store. You enter the store with the intent of stating your position rationally, but your anger takes over pushing you out of control. When you see the damage you are causing, you try to back out of the store. But because you are so unable to channel your anger constructively, you create even more breakage as you attempt to leave.

Hot Head

As a Hot Head you act like you are a pressure cooker which has "popped its lid." You get angry with others for small things because so much pressure has built up from not having dealt with past issues. Others may begin to react to you as if you are a walking time bomb. This stifles their willingness to be genuine with you. Seeing others' responses and sensing their distance further escalates your anger. You then justify your anger even more because of the way people treat you.

23

Godzilla

As Godzilla you play the part of an overgrown monster consumed in your internal rage. You are totally oblivious to others' feelings, so you step on everyone in sight. When you come back through the area later after your anger has subsided, you don't understand why others are doing a damage assessment. You don't realize that you are the cause of the disaster emergency procedures which are now in place.

Inflated Ego Masks

If you choose to wear an inflated ego mask you will need to puff yourself up like a float at the Macy's Thanksgiving Parade. Because you are so large, you will act totally self-absorbed. You will see other people as below you. Seeing others in this way means that you will not develop close connections with them.

Without close connections, you lose touch with your emotions for others. You see emotions as signs of weakness. And weaknesses cannot be tolerated. When you see weaknesses in others, you use them as opportunities to accomplish your own ends.

You will not tolerate weakness in yourself, either. You are afraid that if you show weakness, your inflated ego will pop like a balloon. If you pop, you fear that all that will be left of you is a wet piece of rubber on the ground. Then others will see that you were full of air with no substance.

Top Dog

As Top Dog, you have to be "the winner" in all situations. You see life as a competition, therefore you will do anything to keep from losing. You will even step on your mother if you need to. Since emotions are irrelevant, you rarely notice others' emotions or if you do, you see them as a sign that you have won.

It is difficult for you as Top Dog to have any close friends. Friendship would require you to be a peer, which for you is the equivalent of losing. You may wonder why others do not want to have long-lasting relationships with you. But you don't spend much energy thinking about the why's. Your energy is tied up in being the winner.

Professor

As Professor, you will need to make others feel inferior or stupid. You are condescending and attempt to use your superior knowledge or skills to intimidate others. You use your degrees or experience to degrade others who try to challenge you. Even if your expertise is in a specific area, you may act as the authority in all other areas of your relationships.

As Professor you have an extra wide doorway in your home and office just to accommodate your inflated head. What is inside your head, though, is a secret feeling of stupidity. You might even imagine you really have a pea-sized brain. You think that if you can make others feel less intelligent, it somehow will help you to feel smarter.

Drill Sergeant

As Drill Sergeant, you consider yourself the undisputed authority, demanding respect from all of those around you. You may use degrading tactics to get others to "fall in line" and "kiss your boots." You attempt to "break" others' spirits so they will do anything you ask. No matter how much others grovel to you, though, you never feel like you have enough. This is because you don't respect yourself.

Debater

As Debater, you see your interactions with others in either a "right" or a "wrong" column based on logic. You are like Mr. Spock on Star Trek, without emotions. If others get emotional in an argument, you will attempt to show how illogical their response is. You have a need to make others "wrong" so you can preserve your "rightness."

People close to you may become infuriated with your narrow perception of what is right and your need to view life only through logic. But you see their fury as further evidence that they are "wrong" and flawed human beings. You are able to feel superior to these humanoid defects.

Tough Cookie

As a Tough Cookie, you are like a toasted marshmallow, crusty on the outside and mushy on the inside. The crustiness covers the feeling that something is missing at the core. That *feeling* is correct. Something needs to be solid within to feel safe in the world.

But what you act out to the exterior world is an impenetrable barrier around you so that the mushy core can be disguised or hidden. The energy which must be used to keep the crustiness in place is enormous. Occasionally, someone gets inside the crustiness. Then even more effort must go into reestablishing the crust because an internal warning signal goes off saying, "Warning, warning...Core melt-down danger...Someone is about to get too close...Put all exterior defenses in place now!"

Control Masks

When you choose one of the many control masks, you choose to not take responsibility for the things you really do have control over. Instead you concentrate your energy on the belief that directing others will give your life meaning. To do this, you must "make things happen" outside of yourself. You try to get others to do what you want so that you don't have to do things for yourself.

HIDING BEHIND THE MASK

Orchestra Conductor

As an Orchestra Conductor, you do not play with the others in the orchestra. Instead you act as the master controller of the music. You stand above others. All eyes must be on you before you lift your baton for the playing to begin. When you point at players, they are to play. If you do not point at them, they are to remain silent. Players who make mistakes get "the look" which lets them know they will be in trouble after the performance. You take credit for others playing the music well and blame the players if it was bad.

Backseat Driver

As a Backseat Driver, you do not fully participate in the ride through life, but tell others how to drive their cars. You tell them what to do and where to go. If they choose to take a different route, you berate them for not doing it your way. If the driver gets lost, you say, "I told you where to go, you should have listened to me." If the car breaks down, you tell the owner how to fix it, even though you may not even know what is under the hood. By staying in the backseat, you never take full responsibility for driving your own car. Since you deny yourself the pleasure of living life fully, you compensate by riding vicariously in other people's cars.

Movie Star

As a Movie Star, you see life as a movie set. Life is not real, but only make-believe. You are never your real self. You play whatever starring role you feel will fit the situation to get what you want. You may create a drama, comedy or tragedy, with others in your life playing in bit parts. Whatever the type of movie, you are always the center of attention with others orbiting around you.

Whiner

As the Whiner, you have "Please take care of me." tattooed on your forehead. You think that if you whine like a child, you can manipulate others into getting what you want. "Self-responsibility" is nonexistent in your vocabulary. If anyone tells you they won't take care of you, you tell them they are mean. You sulk, pout, and whine trying to wear them down so they will cave in and treat you better than you are willing to treat yourself.

Sneaky Masks

When you choose to wear a sneaky mask, you find excitement in the midst of turmoil and conflict. You thrive on the intricacy of interactions. You like to plot and scheme. Secrecy gives you a sense of power. But the power you feel is hollow because your sneakiness is an attempt to hide your feelings of inadequacy.

Ambush Renegade

As the Ambush Renegade, you love to set traps for those you are angry with. You are very sneaky and deliberate in your planning because you have revenge as a motive. You have a lot of patience in waiting for just the right moment to make sure that the traps are properly set. You create diversionary tactics if necessary, so that your "prey" will be unaware of your snares. You feel a sense of pride after "bringing in the kill," displaying the heads of those caught in your traps.

Underlying your outward show of pride is a desire to warn others. You do not want them to fall prey to you because you know you are unable to stop your own sneakiness. The only way to stop others from being harmed by you is to let them know your plans.

Snake In the Grass

As the Snake in the Grass, you will need to slink around on your belly, striking at unsuspecting people as they walk by. You will do this just to stir up trouble because you find life dull without conflict or difficulty.

When you see others attending to their bites and wondering who wounded them, you will accuse them of actually having done the deed. You may not accuse the same person every time. You get a thrill out of seeing whether others besides yourself will get blamed. You find excitement in watching confusion and strife between people, especially when you can stand on the sidelines without being blamed for starting the problems.

Backstabbing Confidant

As the Backstabbing Confidant, you act as though you are a friend to others. You encourage them to confide in you and share all of their secrets and perceptions about life. You act to their faces as though you are in complete agreement with them.

Behind their backs, you slip out their secrets to those you think can hurt them. You plant the seeds of mistrust in the minds of their friends. You tell them just enough truth about what has been confided to you that their friends feel betrayed and trust you instead.

"Good" Masks

If you choose to wear a "good" mask, you must be willing to do a lot of self-sacrifice. You believe that if you are "good" you will be rewarded externally for your deeds.

Florence Nightingale

As Florence Nightingale, you spend your energy taking care of other's problems rather than your own. You are the selfless martyr who sacrifices yourself for the outside rewards you get from others. You feel that you will get brownie points in heaven for being "good."

HIDING BEHIND THE MASK

Everybody's Buddy
As Everybody's Buddy, you have an intense desire to be liked by others. You act more like a dog than a human being. You will ask for other's opinions before you tell your own to make sure you do not offend. You will only laugh at jokes that others laugh at first. You will compliment others at every possible turn. You will do "good" things for others hoping that they will notice you and give you a pat on the head.

"Goody" The Two Shoes Wimp
As "Goody" The Two Shoes Wimp, you wimp out on yourself by letting others determine your destiny. You feel that because you are "good," you should be given things and shouldn't have to exert your own effort to get what you want. When things are not handed to you by others, you complain that you have been wronged. But you do not take matters into your own hands. You continue to stand on the street waiting for handouts and wondering why others won't give you what you believe your "goodness" deserves.

Nice Nobody
As Nice Nobody, you are nice and accommodating to others even when they are total jerks or their behavior hurts you greatly. You deny your feelings of hurt or anger. You do not want others to know that you really have such "unnice" feelings. There is a lot vested in having others think

32

that you are without flaws. You would rather be nice and a nobody than to be seen and risk having the real you not loved.

Struggle Masks

If you wear a struggle mask, you must decide what you want but are not willing to give yourself. You are like the mythological character, Sisyphus. You must roll your stone of struggle uphill, but never get to the top.

Busy Bee

As the Busy Bee, you run around in "manic mode," continually *doing* without relaxing. You act like you have one speed...hyperdrive.

You should never stop long enough to see if what you are doing really needs to be done. Also you must never consider that there might be an easier way to do what you are doing. You should not question whether you really want to do something, or whether it feels uncomfortable.

If you ever feel that you are close to running out of things to keep you busy so you could rest, be sure that you make a list of more to do. Or better yet, ask others to give you their chores. The point of keeping busy is not to be happy, but to let yourself and others know that you are indispensable and therefore deserving of recognition and love.

Perennial Procrastinator

As the Perennial Procrastinator, you wait until the last minute to do things so that a struggle will be created. You may like to run late for meetings or keep people waiting. The more people you can pull in around you at the last minute to help you in the struggle—the better. Struggle makes you the center of attention. At least for a short time, because you are the commander telling everyone else how you want the struggle drama to be played out. Like a speedboat going amongst the sailboats, you create a wake that rocks anyone else close by.

Sabotage Specialist

As the Sabotage Specialist you are required to find difficult ways to do things. Especially when there is obviously an easier way. If you could walk in a straight line, you will walk a jagged course just to make it hard on yourself. You love to tell others in minute detail about how difficult the route is that you have taken. You believe that because you have struggled, there is a bigger sense of accomplishment when the task finally is complete. You take great pride in the struggle. If you ever accidently do something easily, you discount the experience as a fluke and forget that it was easy. The only ways that count to you are the difficult ones.

Juggler

As a Juggler, you like to keep as many balls in the air as possible just to show that you can handle anything thrown in your direction. Once a situation has become stabilized, you will ask someone to throw you another ball.

When you have as many balls as you can possibly juggle, you add to your routine by twirling a ring on one leg and then a hoola hoop on your waist. You get a superior feeling from being able to juggle so much at once. You are judgmental toward others who are not willing to do as much as you do. You feel they are slackers.

Amelia "Ear" Heart

As Amelia "Ear" Heart, you play the victim and do not take responsibility for your own issues. Like scout badges, you wear your victimizing struggles on your sleeve as excuses why life is so hard. If anyone asks you why you are making things so difficult, you can point to the badges and "bend their ear" by telling them how the traumas in your life have kept you from being who you could be otherwise.

Grim Grump

As Grim Grump, you must see no joy in life, only blackness. You will want to go around with a frown on your face. You attempt to be a rain cloud on other people's sunny days. Everything that you do is a very serious matter and undertaken in a worklike manner. If others try to cajole you out of your grumpy mood, you will try to bring them down into your misery instead.

To Play or Not to Play, That is the Question

Now that you've seen the games and the masks, do you still want to live life this way? If you decide not to play the games of the mask, you're going to have to look at things differently. **To take off your mask and end the games means that you will have to take responsibility for *your* part in choosing to play the games and choosing your perception about life.**

If you stop even for a short time, you will never again feel completely comfortable in your mask and playing the games. You will start to see the unholy nature and the absurdity that living with a mask has created for you. Stepping outside the games means that you will have to do what it takes to get the happiness and joy you want. And both of them lie beyond the games and the mask.

If you feel you really want to stop living with a mask, read on. But beware! If you want to continue to hide behind your mask, you should put the book down now. Seeing more may only frustrate you and sabotage your enjoyment of wearing your mask.

CHAPTER 4
The Face Revealed

"Come Out, Come Out, Whoever You Are."

We play the games and wear masks because we *believe* we are protecting our tender face beneath. We fear that exposing ourselves means that our very existence will be threatened or harmed. Wearing masks helps us feel protected. But there is a price to pay when living with masks. The barrier we hide behind under the guise of protection smothers the most precious part of us, our essence.

Our essence is like a precious gem which we treasure more than anything else. We will do *anything* we feel we have to do to protect it and keep others from taking or damaging it. We will even deceive ourselves if necessary to keep our essence from harm. In the next chapter we will see how we deceive ourselves for "protection." But now we will examine that precious gem which we so carefully guard.

Our Essence Contains the True Self

Essence is the inward nature of a person, the true substance. It is the sum of the characteristics or qualities that sets one person apart from others. It is our individuality which makes us as unique as delicate snowflakes. Essence is our real face under the mask.

Essence is not about personality, although personality can show us glimpses of someone's essence. It is the intangible part of us which is connected to the whole. Some people call it spirit, core, higher self, or soul. Whatever you call it, your essence is what makes you, *YOU*.

A Look Behind Our Masks

Since we hide our essence with masks, we may have forgotten what it is like. But our essence will always have certain qualities even when we do not acknowledge them. We can choose whether we want to be aware of and act on these attributes or not. The following are some of the features that our essence has:

We have a unique truth.

Essence contains our unique "truth" about reality and our relationship to universal laws. It is part of our blueprint which makes us the interesting human beings that we are. Our truth gives us a special perspective on life that no one else has. It allows us to contribute to the world in a way that only we can do.

Truth is an inner experience. It is something that no one else can give to us because we already have it inside. Outside influence can only confirm or challenge our truth, but can never replace it.

Truth is always there, even when we are not willing to acknowledge it. It may be silenced but never killed, no matter what others do to us, or we do to ourselves to try to deny its existence.

Free will is innately ours.

No matter what system of government we live under, or what our personal circumstances, we each innately are endowed with free will. There is nothing others can do to the *real* us (our essence). Our bodies can be shackled, our intellect can be challenged, our emotions can be toyed with. But only *we* decide how those outside forces influence us and effect our perception. We may be made to do certain things against our wishes, but no one can make us feel internally about ourselves any other way than what we choose to feel.

Free will means that we can choose whether we want to remain free or whether we are willing to allow others to do our thinking for us. There are plenty of examples of people put in isolation or brainwashed in an attempt to "break their spirit" so they would be easy to control. Some people succumbed to the outside pressure and others chose to remain free, internally. It was their choice, as it is our choice. No one can ever control us, unless we choose that internally.

We are innately loving.

Just as we cannot stop our heart from beating or our lungs from breathing, love is an involuntary part of our essence. Love is the glue which connects us to everything. It is the energy which transcends the three-dimensional reality in which most people live.

Love naturally flows in and out of our essence with ease and grace. There is no effort involved in our ability to give or receive love. It is limitless. There is a wellspring within each of us when we tap into the universal supply.

Some people think that there is a finite amount of love available. This is only because they have temporarily forgotten the truth about love. There is always more love available. All we have to do is allow ourselves to feel what is already within us.

We are perfect.

We are each perfect beings just the way we are. Our essence contains no flaws, just as a snowflake cannot be flawed. There is no need to prove our perfection. And we don't need to justify ourselves for being "different" from others. Of course we are different. It cannot be otherwise.

Perfection is not something which is drilled into us by teaching us manners or rules. And it is not something that we can lose, if we go against another person, authority figure, or society.

People often confuse the "perfection of essence" with the "perfection of personality." Our personality is an outward sign of who we are. But personality only reflects our essence to the extent that we are aware of and connected to the real person under the mask. Perfection transcends what we show to the world. It is just naturally a part of us.

We each have a life force.

Emanating from our essence is a life force from which all of our other energy flows. The life force is that spark of power which propels us into humanhood. This force naturally flows throughout our entire being. It is what makes being and doing, like gliding freely on ice skates.

When we stifle the life force by wearing a mask, the force becomes backed up within us. It is like dammed up water looking for an outlet. Eventually it will have to come out, but may not flow where it serves our best interest. Unblocking the life force energy allows us to flow naturally once again.

We are inherently strong.

Being strong is not just a trait that a few select people have. Everyone has strength. Strength to be and do whatever we choose. Strength to make the best of a situation. Strength to overcome seeming obstacles.

We do not have to be heroes and heroines to realize that we are strong. It took a lot of strength for each of us just to be born. And if we have made it to adulthood, we have exhibited our strength in countless small ways to get to where we are.

We are innately open.

As babies we are completely open to learning and showing others who we are. This is because openness is our natural state of being. In an open state we are able to see choices and possibilities unfold before us. When we allow others to truly know us, we are most likely to fulfill our hearts' desires.

Openness allows our essence to come to the surface, so it can guide us through life. When we are directed from within, there is no fear of failure at anything we do because everything is seen as a way to learn something new about other people and ourselves.

We are energy.
All matter in the universe is made up of energy. The form of the energy takes on certain shapes which we see as our three dimensional reality. But energy is not limited to only what we see. As we have all experienced, when we love someone, there is an energy which is transferred which cannot be seen, but is there. We know it exists even though it lies beyond our five senses.

Such is the case with being in the human form. We, too, are pure energy. The form of our energy is unique to us. Like strings on a guitar, we each have energy which vibrates at a different rate. While we do not have "control" over our energy, we can align ourselves with our natural energy vibration. This helps us flow through life rather than being dragged through it kicking and screaming.

We are pure consciousness.
We are not our thoughts. We are not our emotions. We are not our bodies. And we are not our actions. So what are we?

Our essence is pure consciousness which is beyond what we are able to take in through our five senses or what we are able to do with our bodies or minds. When we go beyond our senses and connect with our pure consciousness, we are transformed. We are no longer *human doings*. We are now really *human beings*.

Moving to the "Being" level enables us to experience from a broader perspective. We are able to see endless possibilities, tap into the universal knowledge, experience infinite creativity, discover our full potential, awaken to the perfection of everything around us, and know that we are unbounded and free.

We are able to experience bliss when we acknowledge our pure consciousness. Bliss goes beyond the emotion of happiness. Bliss is perfect ecstasy. It is expressed at every level of our being. Bliss allows our energy to vibrate in synchrony with the universal energy which gives us ultimate peace.

All our answers are contained internally.

We may need to be reminded by outside sources about what we already know. But the fact remains that anything or anyone outside of us only serves to jog our memories. Sometimes others say things which we know not to be true. This also serves to clarify our answers by clearing away the non-answers.

If we are willing to listen to our essence it will always give us an answer in some form. Only we can know the *answer which is uniquely ours*. When it is our answer, we will have an emotional and body sense of having hit the jackpot. We may begin to tingle all over...Get a burst of energy...Want to shout, jump for joy, or cry. There may be an enormous sense of peace which wraps us in a blanket of calm. The verification of the truth will vary from person to person and experience to experience. But there will be an internal sign which helps us know that the answer reflects our truth.

Answers may come in many forms. A co-worker may say something to us at the right time. A passage in a book may remind us of what we had written in a journal, but forgotten. An image in meditation or prayer may guide us to a new perspective we hadn't considered. A letter from a friend may speak directly to the part of us which needs to be encouraged. Or a billboard's message may be the key we needed to spark our creative process. There are infinite ways that our answers reveal themselves to us. But even if the message appears to come from outside of us, it is our *internal ability to see the message as a key* which gives us the answer we were searching for.

We are inherently wise.

Human beings have an amazing knowingness. As a species we have wisdom on many levels which most people are just beginning to understand. Our wisdom extends to the smallest molecules in our microscopic world, all the way out into the universal consciousness.

There is also wisdom in our ability to read ourselves and other people. Everyone has everyone else's blueprint. We really know all there is to know about one another. There are no true secrets. We know how to separate out truth from falsehood and we know what is really coming from the essence and what is coming from another source. We may choose to cover over this wisdom, but it is there waiting to be uncloaked.

Our bodies have wisdom.
Body wisdom is separated into a section by itself because most people are unaware of the immense wisdom which our bodies contain. The wisdom in the body may not be as articulate as other aspects of our essence, but there is a vast amount of knowledge which can guide us, if we allow it to.

We are innately balanced.
We are each born with an internal gyroscope which gives us perfect balance. We are balanced on many levels. Our centers of energy (chakras) are balanced. Our emotions are balanced. Our body is in balance with all its parts. Our breathing is in balance. Our entire system naturally fits together harmoniously to allow us to go through life with grace and ease.

There is no need to struggle when we are operating from our essence. Struggle happens only when we attempt to override our natural balance by thinking that something other than our essence can do it better.

We are innately capable of giving and receiving.
Part of the balance which is contained in our essence is our ability to be both a giver and a receiver. This does not just mean with money, although money is one outward experience which gives us lessons on giving and receiving. But we also have an innate balance of giving and receiving in the areas of emotional support, physical touching, spiritual nurturing, and many other areas.

We only get out of balance with giving and receiving when we deny or ignore our essence. So if we are feeling out of balance on either the giving or receiving end, we are blocking our natural ability.

We are naturally connected to everyone.
The feeling of separation or isolation from others is simply an illusion. We all are connected through love, the glue which holds humanity together. We may choose to block or be numb to our connection, but it is still there waiting for us to reach out and experience it.

We are part of a whole which forms this network of humanity. We each have a unique role to play in this community of people. It is up to us to figure out how we fit into this grand puzzle. When we are connected to ourselves, we are guided to our natural connection with others.

We know what our lessons are.
There are lessons we give to ourselves to learn certain aspects of life. By examining our patterns we

are able to see what the lessons are, so we can get the point and move on to new lessons.

We can choose to understand the lessons or not. If we choose not to resolve a lesson, that is all right, too. We will get another chance at it later. The scenario may look slightly different, but the underlying message will be the same. Just acknowledging that we even have lessons is a first step to owning our truth so it can assist us through life.

We each know what we want to contribute.

We each have special contributions to give to the world and one another. No one else can give exactly what we can, because we are unique.

Much of what our life is about is learning the skills, acquiring the knowledge, and discovering what we need to have as tools to do our part. Our contribution must come from our own truth, or we will constantly be dissatisfied fulfilling someone else's version of what we "should" contribute. A lot of what we learn is weeding out choices which do not fulfill our inner truth's desires. Many times, by process of elimination, we are able to see our true choice standing shining before us.

We are each doing the best we can.

Each of us is doing the best that we can, coming from the level of awareness we have at any given moment. Some people choose to spend an entire lifetime repeating lessons without understanding. They may need the same situation to happen over and over until they hit bottom so they can say, "No more. The pattern ends here." Other people are able to face lessons and go through them very quickly. No one can say what is right for you. And there is no set timetable for all people or a way we "should" learn. This is not meant to be used as an excuse for not facing our issues. It is simply a statement that everyone has their unique pace and methods for discovering their true essence.

When the qualities of our essence are revealed, it is no wonder we are so protective of our gem. Unfortunately, in the effort to protect our essence, we may fall prey to the masks' promises to protect our essence for us better than we can protect it ourselves. Ironically, what we end up doing is sacrificing our essence to save it. Next we will examine how that can be possible.

Part 2
The Lies of the Mask

CHAPTER 5
The Mask's
Lying Contract

"Never mind what it says, just sign here."

When we feel secure about who we are, we know we can take care of our own essence. But being secure within ourselves is not something promoted in our society comprised of so many mask-wearers.

Most of us have been deceived for so long about our truth and essence that we have become brainwashed. We continue to be sucked into the "lies of the mask" because we do not know how to think, feel, or act for ourselves. Our indoctrination is so complete that unless we break the spell of the mask now, we will not only continue to hurt ourselves, we will unwittingly preserve and perpetuate the mask's lies for future generations.

In this chapter, we will expose some of the ways in which we deceive ourselves so that we can agree to play the "games of the mask" and take on roles which do not fit our truth. As we see the false beliefs and painful feelings emerge, we will understand why it feels necessary to cling to a facade to hide behind.

Agreeing to Live by the Contract

Living from behind a mask automatically means that we have agreed to the "mask's lying" at some very deep levels. We are allowing something or someone other than our true self to dictate our behavior, attitudes, values, and feelings. Instead of ignoring anything outside of us and going about our own business, we listen to the lies and decide to act as though they are true.

It is as if the mask gives us an imaginary contract to sign. If we want to play with everyone else (feel connection and camaraderie), we must sign on the dotted line. Because we don't want to be left out, we sign the contract without even reading it to see what we have agreed to.

The only way the "mask's lying contract" can have any effect, is if both parties agree to the lies that their individual masks have created. **If either party does not agree to accept the lie and chooses to stand firm in his or her truth, the "mask's lying contract" falls apart.**

Provisions of the "Mask's Lying Contract" that we agree to:
1. The mask contains the truth about reality. All other perceptions do not count.
2. The mask knows what is best for us. We should ignore all intuition or feelings which contradict what the mask tells us.
3. The mask is all-wise and all-knowing. We do not need to think. If we think that we are wise or know anything, it really means we are stupid or ignorant.
4. The mask is strong, we are weak. We must depend on and draw upon the mask for our strength.

5. The mask is well-rounded and together. We are wounded, scattered, sick, or deluded.
6. Living without the mask can cause us great harm. We are unable to protect ourselves. Without defenses that the mask gives to us, we will be at the mercy of anyone who wants to hurt us.
7. There is no freedom unless the mask grants it to us.
8. Self-responsibility is oppressive responsibility. Giving our personal responsibility to the mask makes our life easy and safe.
9. The mask decides what emotions we are permitted to feel and it will determine how those emotions are allowed to be expressed. If we feel other emotions, there is something wrong with us. We must bury these emotions so that no one will know we have experienced them.
10. Someone must be blamed if things go wrong. The mask only takes responsibility for things perceived as "good." Once the mask assigns blame, we have to go along with the mask's assessment and act as though blame is part of our reality.
11. Life is complicated. The mask must decipher what it all means. It would be impossible for us to figure it out with our simpleton minds.
12. Uniformity of thinking and behaving is permitted. Only the mask decides what is acceptable. All other ideas, thoughts, actions and behaviors are not tolerated by the mask. Nonconformity indicates deviance or mental illness.

13. Individuality is a sign of selfishness and perversion. Only the mask can tell us who we are supposed to be.
14. There are finite resources available to us. All resources are controlled by the mask and must be carefully doled out because we don't have the discretion or discipline to use the resources appropriately.
15. This contract is binding upon the signer. It can only be cancelled by the mask. Any attempt to get out of the contract will cause severe penalties to be imposed, including death if necessary.

_____   _____
Your signature   Date

At the point that we sign the "mask's lying contract," we have unknowingly given ourselves over to a tyrant. If we later attempt to get out of the contract, the tyrant mask will point to the last provision to remind us that the contract is binding.

Self-deceptions Bind Us to the Mask's Lies

If we believe we are stuck with the mask's contract, we will have to twist and contort our perception of ourselves. This attempt to cover over our essence takes an immense amount of "self-deception" energy.

THE LIES OF THE MASK

The mask is willing to plant the seed within us that there is something flawed about our essence. That is the only way it can continue to be in a position of power over the essence. Whenever we start to feel good about ourselves, the mask will whisper in our ear that there is something wrong with us. It is only by continually bombarding us with lies about ourselves that the tyrant mask can keep us brainwashed into believing it has control over us.

Self-deception 1:
We believe we are bad.
We feel that we are flawed as human beings, "bad seeds." When we were punished as children, we may have heard, "You're a bad kid," instead of "That's a bad thing you did." As adults we are still unable to separate our behavior from our essence, so we see our essence as bad.

Because we perceive ourselves as bad, this is what we project onto the world. We attempt to get others to validate our badness by doing and saying things which will get people to dislike us.
Example: Ginger grew up in a very tough neighborhood. She developed a reputation as being the "rotten" kid. She robbed old ladies with a knife, just to see their fear. She smashed car windows with a baseball bat and waited to see the owners' reactions. Now she is an adult. She just got a job at a manufacturing company, on the assembly line. On the first day, she picked a fight

with the woman next to her and purposely put parts on backward to see if anyone would notice. She acts out her bad behavior to tell herself she is a bad person.

Self-deception 2:
We believe something is wrong with us or we are defective.
Twisting our perception of ourselves into what the mask says is true makes us feel like something is desperately wrong. But we mistake the "something is wrong" as emanating from ourselves rather than due to living in an impossible reality created by the mask. Because we feel powerless to turn against the mask, we end up turning against ourselves. When we feel something is wrong with us, we will add another layer to our mask to keep people from seeing who we are.
Example: Frances is a battered wife. She knows something is very wrong. But instead of seeing that it is wrong to be in an abusive relationship, she blames herself. She continues to stay in her marriage with Frank because she feels that there is something wrong with her. She is afraid to leave because she doesn't want anyone else to see her defects.

Self-deception 3:
We believe we are unlovable.
If we think we are bad or something is wrong with us, we may believe that we are unlovable.

Even when other people show us love, we may reject it so we can keep ourselves deluded.

Example: James is dating Cindy. Cindy is very open in her affection for James. Every time she says, "I love you," James flinches. He feels as if a lightning bolt has stabbed his heart. The more Cindy expresses her love, the more James gives her the cold shoulder. Since James feels unlovable, he believes that anyone who tells him he is lovable must be lying to him.

Self-deception 4:
We don't believe it is possible to get love.
We believe love is like a carrot at the end of a stick for us. It is something to strive for, but never obtain. We, therefore, have to keep love at arms length to prove that it isn't possible to get. If someone comes into our life who gives us the love we want, we may sabotage or end the relationship. The game of "push-pull" is a very familiar one.

Example: Alice is always looking for a man to love her. But every time one comes into her life, she finds some excuse why he is not the right one for her. She complains to her friends that love seems to be just a fantasy. She believes that others who say they are in love are simply dreaming.

Self-deception 5:
We believe we are less adequate than others.

We extrapolate the comparison of outward abilities as an indictment on the value of our essence. We don't see our unique qualities as strengths. We instead focus on our weaknesses so that we can put ourselves down. Is it any wonder we buy into this "one up, one down" mentality when we see the tyrant mask as superior to our essence?

Example: Ronnie, who is a great mathematician, hears George play the piano. He thinks, "Look at how George plays the piano. I am less of a person since I can't play the piano as well." Ronnie completely overlooks his mathematical ability as having merit equal to George's skills on the piano.

Self-deception 6:
We feel stupid or unintelligent.

Even though our IQ would say otherwise, we may feel stupid or less intelligent than other people. There is often a comparison between ourselves and others when we put our intelligence down because of our inability to think exactly the same way as others. The fact is that our intelligence is unique. It is demonstrated in many forms besides I.Q. There are those who are considered "eggheads" who couldn't beat their way out of a paper bag in a situation we may find very easy to deal with. But we overlook this fact and choose only to see others as intellectually superior.

Example: Jeannie never got a college degree. She works as an office manager for a large law firm. She always feels stupid when talking to the attorneys. She acts as though they know more about life than she does because they went to law school. She ignores the fact that she has an amazing ability to organize and remember details. All of the attorneys who work with her value Jeannie for her ability to keep the office running smoothly while they do their legal work. No matter how much the attorneys express their appreciation to her, Jeannie still feels stupid around them.

Self-deception 7:
We believe we are unimportant or unworthy.

We feel we must prove ourselves worthy of being here on earth. We have forgotten that if we are alive, we automatically are important and worthy. When we feel unimportant and unworthy, we set ourselves up to fit into others' views of what is important and worthy. When we do this, we suppress what we feel we naturally want to contribute.

Example: Juan's father is an accountant. So are Juan's two brothers. Juan really hates working with numbers even though he has helped out in his father's business since he was 16 years old. His secret love is writing music. But he feels unworthy as a son because he does not want to follow his brothers into his father's profession. Juan stays up nights writing depressing songs about how unworthy he is. He fails to realize that accepting his music as his unique gift is his ticket out of feeling unworthy.

Self-deception 8:
We believe we are untrustworthy.

If we believe we are bad, we will often believe that the bad part of us can't be trusted. We may act out to ourselves or others to prove we are not trustworthy. By betraying others, we reinforce our belief that we are untrustworthy.

Example: Fred is almost always at least 30 minutes late when meeting his wife, Amanda, anywhere. Amanda says that she will not tolerate Fred's being late and will leave without waiting for him if he is more than 15 minutes late the next time they meet for dinner. Fred agrees he will change, but as he walks out of his office on the evening of their next meeting, he finds paperwork which *needs* be done before tomorrow's meeting. Instead of leaving so he can be on time, he decides to do the paperwork which makes him 40 minutes late for dinner. When his wife is not there to meet him, he says to himself, "I knew I couldn't get here on time." Fred sabotaged himself so he could prove that he was untrustworthy.

Self-deception 9:
We believe our perceptions cannot be trusted.

Signing the mask's contract means that we believe we have to sacrifice our reality. So it is no wonder we do not feel we can trust our perceptions. We begin to have great agitation internally due to understanding the world in one way, but living it in another.

Example: Sandra sees her brother molest her sister as she has so many times before. But she no longer acts like anything is wrong when she sees it. She now says to herself, "Oh, Bill was only tickling Barbara." If Sandra thinks about what really happens to Barbara, she is afraid her anger will make her kill her brother. Denying her perception of the situation seems preferable to expressing her rage. But it doesn't make the *feeling* of rage go away.

Self-deception 10:
We believe we must live a life of suffering.

Attempting to live our life the way someone else wants us to live it, rather than the way we want, automatically means that we will not be going with our natural flow. Going against our natural inclinations makes us very angry. In our self-anger we punish ourselves by suffering. It is the only way we know to keep doing something other than what we want to do.

Example: Mabel suffers from chronic back pain and heart problems. She suffers because she sees her children "wreck" their lives. She suffers because she has had an unhappy marriage for 50 years and has never gotten the love she really wanted. Mabel is a life-long sufferer who feels that life is passing her by because she has never enjoyed life or gotten to do what she really wanted to do.

Self-deception 11:
We don't believe there is enough to go around.

We have a belief that there is lack in the world. Lack of money, lack of support, lack of love, lack of resources, lack of opportunities, and so on. There is a lack of everything—except lack. This is a very insidious belief because lack is exactly what we will draw to ourselves, if that is what we believe. Lack also fuels our self-doubts and fear of the world. We feel there is a "not enoughness" within ourselves, so we are afraid to show the world who we are. We do not want to be ridiculed for lacking wholeness.

Example: Beverly is a hairdresser who is always without money. No matter how many extra clients she sees, she never has quite enough money to pay the rent and her car payment. She sees herself as lacking skills to get a better paying job. She feels depressed because she lacks a boyfriend. Beverly doubts that she will ever have a better life because she doesn't believe she has enough substance for her to ever amount to much.

Self-deception 12:
We believe we are trapped.

Believing the mask's lies boxes us into a world that is not our own. We may feel like caged animals without realizing the reason. We don't give ourselves freedom to explore other options because we believe our whole world might fall apart. To maintain this view, we must keep ourselves narrowly focused on how things "have to be." We reject alternative perceptions in order to remain trapped in the illusory cage.

Example: Wayne works at a job he hates. He believes he has no option but to stay. He has a house with a mortgage and two kids, with another on the way. He wants to change fields, but feels trapped by all the obligations. He gets depressed thinking that he has no options. Because Wayne feels so trapped, he does not bother to update his resume, take classes, or even talk to others about his true desires. He closes out all possibilities by his unwillingness to entertain alternate perceptions.

Self-deception 13:
We act as if we do not have courage.

The desire to avoid pain is an underlying reason that it is difficult for us to access our courage. We believe that if we feel the pain of our issues, it will hurt so badly that the pain will

THE MASK'S LYING CONTRACT

never end. Because we have not yet experienced the *release which comes from leaning into the pain*, we do not know there is joy on the other side. So the very thing that we so desperately avoid, perpetual pain, is exactly what we get. The mask is always ready to tell us that courage will bring pain with even greater intensity.

Example: Lucinda's heart's desire is to be an Olympic ice skater. She knows deep down that she has what it takes to make a champion, except for one thing. She lacks courage. She is afraid that if she begins competing, she will not make the cuts. She is so fearful of not reaching her goal, that she holds herself back so she won't be disappointed. When Lucinda fails to push through her fear, she doesn't see that she has an immense amount of courage which can take her all the way to the top.

The "mask's lying contract" is well on its way to becoming a reality when we are willing to deceive ourselves. The mask can coast along simply reminding us periodically of the contract we signed while we continue to brainwash ourselves.

CHAPTER 6
Playing Bullies and Victims: Acting Out the Mask's Lies

"If I've flogged you once, I've flogged you a thousand times."

The "mask's lying contract" remains only a grotesque idea until we agree to play roles to actualize the contract. This can become a bizarre live game. Because the mask has to act like a bully to get us to live out the contract, it is no wonder that the game of "bully/victim" is a cornerstone of the mask's contract. If everyone operated from their truth and ignored the mask's lies, the contract would dissolve into oblivion. **The only way that the mask's contract has meaning is when we choose to give life to the provisions of the contract.**

Behavior Versus the Real Person

When we encounter someone whose behavior is bullying or that of a victim, we can be sure we are not seeing the real person. We are instead seeing a "bully" or "victim" mask. This is a defensive covering to protect the person beneath the mask who has been wounded and brainwashed by the lies of the mask. We may be experiencing bullying *behavior* but the actual *person* is not a bully. We may be seeing someone *acting* like a victim but the actual *person* is not a victim. This distinction is very significant because it is that very confusion which allows us to buy into the "mask's lying contract" and the game of "bully/victim."

Opposite Sides of the Same Coin

People who play at being bullies and victims have many similarities. They each wear masks to hide their true identity from the world. They each use self-deception to live by the "mask's lying contract." And they each are so enmeshed in the game that they are unable to see that they are even playing the game of "bully/victim." The difference between the two is only in the way that the self deception is played out in their view of themselves and others in the world. Thus, the bully and victim roles are simply opposite sides of the same coin. An internal flip of the coin can make a bully into a victim or a victim into a bully. But as long as they flip back and forth between bully and victim, they stay trapped on the face of the coin, never living beyond a self-imposed prison.

Deciding Between
Bully and Victim Masks

How people decide which side of the bully/victim coin to be on is something which is very individualistic and will need to be explored on a case by case basis. But there are some common factors which go into the decision whether to play out the exterior bully or victim roles. Some of the differences are:

How truth is sacrificed

Both bullies and victims sacrifice their truth to play the "games of the mask."

Bullies sacrifice their truth for "power" over others. They deny their feelings and the feelings of others. They attempt to make others as uncomfortable as they are themselves. They forget what they really know so they can deny responsibility for their own issues.

Victims sacrifice their truth to get along with others. They deny their reality in an effort to keep others from feeling uncomfortable. They forget what they really know so others won't have to face their own truth.

Whose false reality is believed

Both bullies and victims believe and act from a false reality of their mask instead of dealing with life from their truth.

Bullies believe that their reality must be everyone's reality. They demand that others act as though theirs is the "right" reality even when others have a difference of opinion. Conformity to their belief system gives bullies a sense of false security. If they can get others to agree with them, then they *must* be right.

Victims are willing to suspend (or pretend to suspend) their reality to go along with the bully's reality. They do this to get along, be loved, be cared for, or not have to decide for themselves. Conformity to another's belief system feels comforting to victims because they can pretend that someone else is in charge of their lives.

Who gets blamed

Both bullies and victims look for someone to blame for how they are. They do this to weasel out of self-responsibility for thoughts, feelings and actions.

Bullies blame anyone and everyone for how they are when they don't like something. Bullies search for a scapegoat. They are always able to find others besides themselves, even if they have to get very creative to find someone.

Victims act to bullies' faces as if they accept the blame that the bullies dump on them. But by doing this they are able tell everyone else behind the bullies' backs that their victimization is due to how shabbily they are treated by the bully.

Where attention is focused

Both bullies and victims focus attention on playing out the "games of the mask" rather than on their individual truth. Their energy is so consumed in games playing that there is little left to nurture the real person.

Bullies act as if they are the center of attention. All others are supposed to orbit around them. Everyone's energy is focused in their direction. Bullies will sacrifice others' feelings or rights so they can maintain their starring role.

THE LIES OF THE MASK

Victims act like supporting players and stage hands. They cater to the bullies' starring roles. Victims' attention is given up to the bullies. They look for ways to make bullies feel good or right. Some victims will sacrifice their entire self, if necessary, to accomplish this. Victims do not want to be in the starring role, because to be out there would expose their flaws for the world to see and attack.

Where the self is perceived in a "hierarchy"

In accepting the "mask's lying contract," the world must be seen as a hierarchy of people. There has to be someone higher and someone lower in status, ability, worthiness, etc. This "pecking order" must be maintained for there to be bullies and victims. The hierarchy cannot be exposed for the illusion that it really is, or people would know they were peers, no higher or lower than anyone else.

Bullies act as if they are higher than others in the hierarchy. This way they can feel superior and not have to face the fact that they have human flaws and foibles just like those around them. Denial of flaws and foibles is a must because bullies do not want to face themselves.

Victims act as if they are lower than others in the hierarchy. This way they can pretend that they are inferior. By doing this they don't have to face the fact that they are just as capable as anyone else for living their lives however they want.

How the self is defended

Bullies and victims both need to defend themselves since they do not feel comfortable showing their true selves.

Bullies act as though offense is the best defense. They see things in terms of attack. If they can attack others, maybe no one will see who they really are and try to hurt them.

Victims act as if retreat is the best defense. They see the world around them as a scary place with someone ready to attack them behind every tree. They tie up their energy in looking for places to retreat so they won't be confronted with who they really are.

What is acted out instead of assertiveness

Neither bully nor victim act assertively because they don't know how.

Bullies generally behave aggressively. They attempt to do things by force, whether it is physical force or verbal force. They try to *make* things happen.

Victims generally behave passively. They attempt to stay out of the way of the bully's force. They hope things will happen *for* them.

How the self is portrayed to others

Since both bully and victim wear masks, they hide their true selves from others.

Bullies attempt to look stronger than they actually are. They are afraid that others will see them as weak, so they pump themselves up like a bullfrog to protect themselves. Their boundaries often extend into other people's space.

Victims attempt to look weaker than they actually are. They are afraid that they will be a threat to others if they show their strong selves. They squeeze themselves down as if living in a sardine can. Their boundaries are often so collapsed that others are easily able to intrude on their space.

How to get what is wanted

Both bullies and victims seek outside of themselves to get what they want. They think that if others give them what they want they will feel better about themselves.

Bullies try to make others give to them by demanding such things as respect, loyalty, or material offerings. They set themselves up to be like stone gods in the jungle. Natives are supposed to bring sacrifices to them so that wrath of these gods will not be incurred.

Victims try to get others to give to them by hoping, promising, cajoling, or agreeing. They will crawl long distances on their bellies if they think that it will get others to give them what they want.

Where the control is

Both bullies and victims have a need to look outside themselves for control because they feel out of control in their own lives.

Bullies look for weaknesses and flaws in others, as a way to control them. Bullies believe that if they can control others it will show the world and themselves that they are really together, in charge of their lives.

Victims look for weaknesses and flaws in themselves as a way to offer control to others. Victims believe that if they can give enough control away, they will be taken care of by others. Then they won't have to face the fact that they are not willing to take charge of their own lives and take care of themselves.

Acting Like Bullies

*"Bullies may feel powerful, but they
do not feel accepted or loved."*
Lillian Katz, Ph.D.

A bully is defined as a person who hurts, frightens, or tyrannizes those who are smaller or weaker. We are used to talking about bullies in the context of children. The terms "neighborhood bully" and the "schoolyard bully" are well-known. But we rarely talk about the role of bullying behavior in the adult world. Instead we talk about "power games," "ego trips," "politics," "we're number one," "that's just the way it is," "this is reality, take it or leave it," etc. Most of us let ourselves become conditioned into "coping" with situations or developing the behavior of people we actually abhor because it is easier to play games than to figure out another way to live.

Some kinds of bullying are more socially acceptable than others. This depends on what circles one moves in. But the social acceptability of the bullying behavior does not make it any healthier. At a deep level we each know when we are accepting the "mask's lying contract," and it doesn't feel good.

Physical Bullying
The object of physical bullying is to hurt, frighten, intimidate, or wear down people's will so they will be easy to control. It requires making others fear for their physical safety. Superiority of size, physical strength, or weapons are often used or threatened to further terrorize people.

Examples of physically bullying individuals:
•Hitting a spouse
•Spanking a child
•Mugging someone in a dark alley
•Kidnapping
•Rape

Examples of physically bullying groups:
•Robber holding up a bank full of people at gunpoint
•Terrorist hijacking an airplane
•Withholding food from prisoners of war to get them to confess

Mental Bullying
Mental bullying is hurting, frightening or tyrannizing people's *thinking* reality. Our thinking reality takes in information from all the senses and processes the data through our internal knowledge of the world.

PLAYING BULLIES AND VICTIMS

Mental bullying may produce more long-term scars than physical bullying because it damages at deeper levels than just physically. It questions peoples' thinking processes which are so crucial to feeling a strong sense of individuality. Those who feel bullied already feel weak in some portion of their thinking reality. People who mentally bully others sense this and kick them while they are down so that they question even further their internal reality. When their sanity is questioned, people being bullied may feel it necessary to suspend their own reality and try to adopt that of those who bully them.

Example of mentally bullying another person:

A boss could attempt to mentally bully a subordinate who questioned an earlier directive if he said, "Jim, I never gave you that order. I would never say such a thing. What makes you think a thing like that?"

Example of mentally bullying groups of people:

The President of the U.S. could attempt to mentally bully the general public if his campaign slogan was: "NO NEW TAXES." Then when in office, he says in a news conference, "My opponents have been spreading a vicious lie. I have consistently said that I did not favor an *income tax* increase. But it is obvious that we will have to raise other types of taxes."

Emotional Bullying

Emotional bullying is hurting, frightening or tyrannizing people's *feeling* reality. If emotional bullying is consistently done to people over time, they may quit feeling, become numb, or mistake the emotion really being felt for another emotion. This may include feeling anger, but expressing sadness. Or the person being bullied may indeed feel the emotion, but then feel guilt and self blame for having that feeling.

Example of emotionally bullying another person:

Arthur says to his son, Benjamin, "Young man, quit your crying right now. That is nothing to cry about."

Example of mentally bullying groups of people:

Mrs. Flynn is a teacher who has just made a fool of herself in class. She turns beet red. She shouts to the class, "I want you to quit laughing. There is nothing funny here. Wipe those smiles off your faces or you'll all get an F in my class."

Spiritual Bullying

Spiritual bullying is hurting, frightening or tyrannizing people's core truth about themselves and their belief systems.

Spiritual bullying can be very overt such as a preacher telling a congregation, "You are going to burn in hell for your evil ways." But it can be much more subtle, such as when a parent doesn't allow a musically talented child to develop that talent.

Spiritual bullying hasn't been talked about much in our society but the damage to individuals can be very devastating. Prolonged spiritual bullying can cause people to deaden their passion for life. Once passion is dead, all the rest of life is hollow, like being in a numbed state and operating on automatic pilot.

Example of spiritually bullying another person:

Rosalyn says to her son, Roger, "I hate looking at you. You look just like your father and I hate your father's guts. He is a worthless bum and you're turning out just like him."

Example of spiritually bullying groups of people:

Bill is a boot camp drill sergeant. He says to the new recruits, "You are the scum from the bottom of my shoe. You aren't fit to live on this earth. But I'm going to make you *act* like men even though you aren't."

Hero Worship of the Bully

Hero worship of the bully is pervasive in our society. The popularity of such characters as Rambo, Clint Eastwood, James Bond, Terminator, John Wayne, and more recently, Teenage Mutant Ninja Turtles, signify this. Many have argued that these figures are only symbols of good triumphing over evil. The fact remains that all that has been done is to switch roles. The former bully is now bullied by the "good guy." One person is still down while another is up. There is now just a different player who has come out on top.

Bullying Under the Guise of Love

Part of the reason we hero worship the bully is our belief that, "Right justifies might." It is still a cornerstone of our view of reality. The underlying premise is that bullying others can be a loving gesture, if it is done for good purposes. This attitude is very pervasive in our culture. The phrase, "Spare the rod, spoil the child," came out of the belief that if we hit a child, it can be a way to show our love.

We see many authority figures who believe that part of their role is to bully others into doing what is good for them. Judges order community service as punishment for crimes. Doctors keep patients in the hospital even when patients want and are able to leave.

As a nation, we have attacked other countries by saying it was for the good of another nation or the world. Whether you agree or not with a particular position politically, the fact remains that this clearly shows that as a nation our belief is that bullying can be a good thing if it is used for the right reasons.

The "might is right" attitude sends clear signals to ourselves and our children. It says that "if you say you love someone, its okay to bully them as long as you can justify it to yourself in the name of love and enough people agree with you."

Acting Like Victims

"No one can make you feel inferior without your consent."
Eleanor Roosevelt

People who decide to play the victim role agree to read the "script of lies" and take directions from someone else rather than their own truth. Victims play the part of the wounded one, the sick one, the small one, the deluded one, the stupid one, or the silly one. They act out the "poor me" role.

Victims are able to recount their history in great detail, as to how they have been victims their entire lives. They can proudly point to each incident that "happened" to them as if they were talking about their scout badges.

Victims can become very attached to the role over time, having forgotten who they truly are. So they use fear to stay victims. They convince themselves that they fear the wrath of the mask. **In fact what they really fear is facing their truth and calling the lies of the mask for what they are. Victims fear their freedom from their role.**

Part of the "mask's lying contract," which we accept when taking on the victim role, is that the contract is permanently binding. With that provision, only the mask can break the contract. If victims decide at some point not to play the role anymore, they are shown the contract they agreed to. It is pointed out that any attempt to get out of the contract will cause severe punishment. The irony, of course, is that victims can get out of the contract any time they want. Nothing can stop them except their belief that they are hooked for life.

Hurting Our Bodies

The body is our haven. It contains our essence. If we feel safe within our body, then we will feel safe about exploring the realm of emotional, mental and spiritual growth. If our body feels unsafe, we will be preoccupied with survival because, without our body remaining alive, it feels to us like all else will be moot.

Most of us were taught, however, not to trust our bodies. We were encouraged to override the body's understanding of the world and ourselves. The natural things our body knows are covered over by what others have told us. As children, we were told to trust adults who "knew better." As we get older, we still carry the feeling that our bodies cannot be trusted. Some people have taken the feeling to an extreme, viewing the body only as a machine or a vessel for carrying the head. These views deny the fact that our body contains valuable knowledge and can be our partner in discovering our truth if we let it be.

Hurting and victimizing our bodies is one of our favorite pastimes. We spend a lot of energy (and money) to hurt our bodies, so we can hide our real selves and keep our truth buried.

There is ritual and decorum around body victimization which has been built into our society. We gather so we can victimize ourselves together and even gloat to one another about who outdid whom in hurting ourselves. We go to "all you can eat" food orgies and stuff ourselves in gluttony. We go to sporting events and drink alcohol to excess and stumble around in a mental fog. Society dictates to us how we are to hurt ourselves by telling us what is "proper" and "acceptable." Conformity is stressed because if we all victimize our bodies together, there is no one to remind us that we are hurting ourselves.

There are so many ways to victimize our bodies that it would be impossible to look at all of the creative ways that human beings have devised to do it. Included here are a few of the ways in which we commonly hurt our bodies.

Examples of common ways we hurt our bodies:
- Overeating, bulimia, anorexia
- Denying ourselves enough sleep
- Over- or under-exercising
- Addiction to caffeine, alcohol, drugs, sex
- Bombarding (overstimulating) ourselves with noise and sights
- In the name of beauty—piercing ears and noses, tummy tucks, tattoos, artificial tanning

- Wearing uncomfortable clothes—tight pants, high heels, neck ties
- Shallow breathing
- Self-mutilation—biting fingernails, slashing wrists, cutting on self
- Having repeated accidents

Using Our Thoughts Against Ourselves

Mental bullying questions our thinking reality. When we choose to mentally victimize ourselves, our mask plays mind games with us to see if we will buy into its lies. It uses our thoughts as weapons against us.

This is only possible when we are not in touch with our truth. When we know ourselves, we have a solid foundation which no one, not even a very smart mask, can shake by attempting cheap tricks of the mind.

Examples of common messages whispered in our ears by our mask in hopes that our thoughts can be used against us:

- "Stupid, stupid, stupid. I can't ever get anything right."
- "I can't believe I was such a ding-a-ling."
- "What's wrong with me? I must have a screw loose."
- "I must be crazy to think a thing like that."
- "What did I do that for? I am such a sniveling idiot."
- "I'm too helpless to do that."

•"There I go again, being weird."
•"I always crack under pressure. I can never count on myself."
•"I'm so lazy."
•"I can't be trusted."

Emotionally Wounding Ourselves
When we emotionally victimize ourselves, it hurts our feeling reality. It is a way to control us. If we can be made to feel numb or confused about our emotions, then we begin to live like wind-up dolls, going in directions decided by others.

The only way we can be emotionally victimized is if we deny our true feelings and relegate them to a life of exile. It is not that we don't have feelings. We simply have stuffed them down. Without our *real* feelings, we lose touch with our true selves and doubt our reality.

When our feelings are in exile, we are subject to the whims of a mask, whether it is our own or someone else's. Wounding ourselves emotionally is like wearing a neon sign saying, "Please hurt me." If we are willing to pick at our wounds, those who bully say, "Sounds like fun. I think I'll take you up on the offer."

Examples of ways we let our mask pick on us to emotionally wound us:
•"Don't feel it. Don't *even* think it."
•"I must be very sick to feel that!"
•"Ignore those feelings. They'll go away."
•"I'm too old to cry about a thing like that."

•"I can't feel that. It hurts too much."
•"I don't feel a thing."
•"That didn't hurt my feelings."
•"I don't feel any anger."
•"This is not a laughing matter. It is very serious."
•"What have I got to be so happy about?"

Spiritually Maiming Ourselves

We spiritually maim ourselves when we are disconnected from our essence or believe that our truth has no value. We do further spiritual damage to ourselves if we believe that we are not connected to something greater than the masks of ourselves or others.

If we see God as an external concept which can be credited or blamed, we can also spiritually harm ourselves. We make God become part of our mask rather than owning our responsibility for playing out our *perception* of God.

As spiritual victims, we may feel like we are in the middle of an ocean of futility clinging to the sides of a mask which is shaped like a life raft. Prolonged spiritual abuse can deaden us and make us lose passion for life. Without passion life feels meaningless and dull.

There are many ways we creatively devalue our truth and spiritual connection. Here are a few of the ways we do it:

1. We deny our needs & desires.

We may act like we are needless and desireless. Because we really do have needs and desires we try to attach ourselves to others who we feel have "valid" ones. Or we may become numb, and stuff our needs and desires even further down inside us.

2. We put ourselves last.

This is a very common one among those who are champions at spiritual victimization. We may do this in small ways like always choosing the video movie our partner wants to see, but we don't like. We may fix all meals for the family no matter how tired we are without asking for assistance. Or we may do volunteer community service instead of taking the dance class we always wanted to take.

3. We deny our creativity.

We may have so completely suppressed our creativity that we feel that we are not creative people. When our natural creativity is squelched, our passion for life becomes deadened. This is especially true, if we are doing everything else except what gives us passion. Some examples of this are:

    a. Shannon really is a poet at heart, but does electrical engineering as a career because it is considered by her family as a worthy profession.

b. Janet has a love and genius capability in science, but runs a day care center because she thinks she "should" be a caregiver.

c. Jim is a very good cartoonist, but feels he could not make a living at it so he works at a fast food restaurant instead.

4. We disconnect from our hearts.

When we stop loving ourselves, it is difficult to love others or feel strongly about life. We become like Ebenezer Scrooge with a sour disposition. Or we may become a "talking head" simply carried around by our body, but numb to anything but logic and reason. Disconnecting from our heart takes a great deal of effort. Our heart is always there attempting to reopen us to the reality of self-love, connection to others, and universal love.

5. We hold back our passion.

Whether our passion is creativity, sexuality, or excitement for life, when we are playing the spiritual victim, we hold ourselves back. We are like racehorses at the starting gate, waiting for something outside of us to let us go. Since we are not in touch with our life force and truth, we act as though expending our passion will mean that we will be depleted. As spiritual victims we will not let ourselves realize that our passion is like an underground spring, continually giving us as much passion as we are willing to show to the world.

Examples of verbal "darts" with which we spiritually maim ourselves:
• "I don't deserve love."
• "I'm worthless."
• "I'm not very creative."
• "I don't feel any love for myself or anyone else either."
• "Nobody will notice me. Why should they?"
• "I'm so ashamed of myself."
• "I can never forgive myself for that."
• "I am a bad person."
• "There is nothing worth living for."
• "I have made a total mess of my life. It has been a waste."

The Role of Shame in the Game of "Bully/Victim"

Shame is the act of making others feel bad to manipulate their feelings or behavior. It is a tool used often by those who bully. The intent of shaming is to get people to conform to a certain reality other than the one they naturally have. Attempting to shame others is only necessary when one's own personal reality has a shaky foundation. If one's reality is solidly grounded in truth, there is no need to manipulate anyone else through shame.

Shame can only be given to others if they are willing to take it. Shame is like a ball of energy. If the ball is tossed by the senders, but the receivers refuse to accept the shaming energy, it falls flat. It is then up to the senders to decide what to do with the shame ball. Without a sense of completion, senders of shame have several options. They may attempt to throw the shaming energy again to the same receiver to see if this time it will be taken. Or they can find someone new to give it to. Or they can examine why they need to send shaming energy. They can choose to make the internal changes necessary to stop shaming others.

Recently, there has been reference to some shame in codependency literature, as healthy shame. Healthy shame has been described as others reminding us that we are not God and that we have a relationship to people in this world. But this is not shame at all. Knowing that we are not God and that we have relationship in the world does not require any shaming. It does require a broader perspective of the universal laws to see that we are a part of the whole, yet have wholeness within ourselves. Shaming others for not having that perspective does not change their perspective. It only makes them feel bad about the perspective they have.

There is no place for "healthy" shame in anyone's wholeness. Shame is simply a bullying behavior manufactured to get others to validate reality externally instead of looking to individual internal reality.

The Role of Guilt in the Game of "Bully/Victim"

Guilt is what is felt by people on the receiving end of the "shame energy ball" when they accept and hold onto the energy. It is solidified shame. Guilt energy starts settling into the emotional and body memory of receivers and weighs them down until they feel like they are filled with cement.

The receivers agree to guilt because they have accepted the provision in the "mask's lying contract" which states that only the mask is responsible for good feelings. The receivers, whether they play out the bully or the victim role, feel responsible for bad feelings. Guilt is, therefore, a feeling of responsibility for the bad feelings or unresolved issues of ourselves or others.

Guilt implies taking on more responsibility for others than actually exists. But guilt often is a cover for not taking responsibility for our own issues. We are copping out on ourselves. When we entangle our energy in guilt, we can avoid looking at the issues within us that need to be addressed. Guilt consumes our energy like a black hole. It gives us the illusion that we are doing something helpful or loving. In fact we use guilt to avoid facing our own truth. Guilt allows us to continue to live with the lies we have accepted and falsely lived from behind our masks.

The Role of Blame in the Game of "Bully/Victim"

As we discussed earlier, blaming is one of the provisions of the "mask's lying contract." It keeps our energy bound into looking for someone or something to dump our issues on. Our focus becomes directed *outward* on people and things we have no control over instead of where we can really effect a change.

And why do we buy into this provision of the lying contract? Because avoiding responsibility is what we have learned all our lives. We see countries blame one another for their current economic situations. We see ethnic groups blame one another for their present plight. We see our parents blame one another for feeling out of sorts. We learned that *we* don't have to be responsible. Someone else can be made to be responsible, if we search long enough.

Blaming has become an ingrained habit. If we stopped spending our time on blaming, we might be faced with seeing our part in situations. Most people don't want to look at themselves or find solutions. They would rather play the game of "bully/victim" to avoid stirring things up inside.

The Role of Fault-finding in the Game of "Bully/Victim"

Fault-finding is very close to blame in the way we expend our energy. We can spend an inordinate amount of time looking for someone's flaws and assigning fault to them. This enables us to blame that person for our reaction to them.

Looking for faults is a way to pick a person apart like a vulture at a desert feast. Picking on someone else's faults is saying, "See, you have faults that I don't. So, I'm better than you." It's a way to feel superior to the person being picked on. What our dissecting of others really says is, "If I look long enough here, I'll find a part of you I can blame for my feelings and perception of the world." In other words, we use fault-finding as a way to deny our personal responsibility for our own issues.

Finding fault is not the same as seeing people for who they truly are. There is judgment involved in finding fault. Judgment is not present when we simply observe a whole person. Observation shows weaknesses *and* strengths, but there is no need to pick on the weaknesses.

Understanding that Victimization is a Choice

It is difficult for many people to accept, but long term victimization is a choice. Some people get very angry when they hear this. They don't want to believe that they have chosen to do something so hurtful to themselves for so long. They also get angry because when they are in the middle of victimization, it is hard to see that there is a choice.

THE LIES OF THE MASK

Hearing that they can choose something else makes victims feel that they are being further victimized. It is true that to fully get over feeling like victims, we may need to go through a period of *fully* feeling like we were victimized. We need to know, to our core, that we did not deserve the treatment we got. This period of healing may vary in length from person to person. It should not be discounted. It is by owning the real feelings we have that we can let go of them and move on. Only we know the truth of whether we are in a healing phase or if we have crossed over into using our victimization to stop us from living our life the way we are meant to live it.

There are all kinds of reasons we can manufacture to justify why there is no choice for our long suffering victimization. There is a lot of blaming we can do about it. We can say that it is his fault, her fault, my rough childhood, society's fault, men's fault, women's fault, the situation's fault, or the kitchen sink's fault. But placing blame only gives our power away and ties us into the "mask's lying contract." It is only by extracting our energy from all of the bully/victim minutia that we are able to choose to be free of our mask.

Even as children, we have choices about our perception. For instance, in the same family with more than one child and an abusive parent, different children view the abuse in different ways. George may have taken in all of the shaming words which were told to him by Mom. He personalized them. He began to think that he was a bad person. His sister, Sarah, was able to see in the midst of being beaten or yelled at by Mom that Mom's hitting and yelling at her was "that Mom going at it again." Sarah knew that the abuse was not her fault and it had nothing to do with her.

As an adult, George sees his abusive childhood as a trauma which ruined his life. He feels immobilized and attributes his not holding down a steady job to his "bad" childhood. Sarah sees her childhood as something that helped her understand that other people have problems and need help. She sees her experience as giving her compassion for other people in abusive situations.

There are many adults like Sarah who use their childhood situations as the "grist for the mill" to rise above circumstances which would seem to hold others down. These people *choose* not to be victims. They are able to let abuse roll off them, realizing that abuse says nothing about them. To them abuse only shows the masks of those who abuse.

By stating that we have choices about our victimization, some people might think what is being said is that victims are at fault for their situation. This is not the case. Part of playing the game of "bully/victim" is believing that there is blame. **Blame is an illusion created by the mask to keep us sidetracked from finding our truth. Believing that there must be blame is buying into the "mask's lying contract." There is no fault, only situations to be learned from.**

THE LIES OF THE MASK

How we choose to perceive a situation determines whether we *feel* like a victim.

Another example may further clarify this point. Two women are raped in separate instances, but similar scenarios. Sheila hangs on to the rape scene for years, feeling angry, violated, hostile and desiring revenge. She blames society for allowing people like the rapist to exist. She hates all men because of what one man did to her. She hangs on to the rape as one of her badges to show that "life has done her wrong." She *feels* like a victim.

Jill, who was also raped, may have gone through all of the same feelings as Sheila did right after the incident. She, too, felt like a victim at first. She, too, felt angry, violated, hostile and desiring revenge. But she was able to put the rape behind her after a period of time.

Jill was able to do this because she *fully* dealt with her feelings and beliefs. She was willing to dive down to the root of her pain, anger, and fear so they could be released.

Jill is now no longer tied into the rapist's energy by dwelling on it. She does not hang on to blame, so she does not hate all men for the actions of one man. She goes on with her life a stronger person for the insight she gained by seeing the rapist for the person he was. She knows that she is blameless. She feels good about herself because she did not let the rapist's intrusion on her body ruin her life. She sees the incident as a lesson for her that no matter what others do to her physically, she will not let it say anything about her as a person. She chooses to speak out about her situation to expose rape for the violation of another that it is. Is she a victim? Not if she doesn't *feel like one*.

As Jill illustrates, when we take responsibility for our own feelings and perceptions about our interactions with people we stop feeling like victims. Many people get stuck right there and end up mucking endlessly in their victimization. They are unwilling to accept self-responsibility for their *current* feelings and perception about past situations. They know that to do that would require self-examination and that is something they are afraid to do. They would rather continue to blame others so they can divert energy away from facing themselves. If these people would raise their heads above the muck, they could see that blaming others and feeling like victims only ties them even tighter to the "mask's lying contract."

Taking Bullies Off the Pedestals

We may not like bullying behavior. But because there is such reverence in our society for bullies, we may put them on a pedestal like mythical gods and goddesses. If we act out bullying behavior, we may have put ourselves on a pedestal. But pedestals are dangerous places to be because they can be knocked over at any time. Without firm footing on the ground, bullies are likely to fall on their faces.

Seeing bullying as a pretense, helps us see the authentic people beneath the facades of the bully personas. Seeing people for who they truly are makes us less susceptible to such games that bullies and victims love to play. If we are not in the middle of the games, it is much easier to be compassionate toward people who bully. We are more able to come from our own strength in dealing with them. Then when bullying behavior confronts us, we can accept the challenge to understand ourselves and the other person at a deeper level. Rather than knocking the pedestals out from under people, we can give a helping hand. We will then all be on the same level to stop living out the "mask's lying contract" through the game of "bully/victim."

Compassion Does not Excuse Unacceptable Behavior

Seeing the masks that people wear helps us see others as caricatures of the people they really are beneath. This can help us not to get hooked into the games and more easily stay within our own reality. When we start to see people this way, it is also easier to see them for the scared hurt people they really are. In turn, this allows us to love the real person beneath even though we do not like their behavior. Loving the real person behind masks enables us to deal with them from strength: discouraging their behavior, but honoring their wounds.

Understanding bullying and victim behavior gives us compassion for our wounds. But this is *not to be used as justification or excuses for the behavior.* Ultimately we are all still responsible for our own *current* behavior, no matter what happened to make us the way that we are.

Beginning to End the Game of "Bully/Victim"

Seeing bully and victim behavior for what it is takes the first step toward freedom from the "mask's lying contract." To cut through the lies of the mask requires that we also understand and *change* the dynamics of playing the "bully/victim game." In the next chapter we will see how bullies and victims use manipulation and gullibility to actualize their game.

CHAPTER 7
Manipulation and Gullibility: Feeding the Mask's Lies

"If you'll believe this, you'll believe anything."

Preying on people's gullibility has been used through the ages to control people. Gullibility can be used on a grand scale such as Hitler did. He played on the blind faith of the German people to follow him. He got them to destroy millions of people and entire countries to further his desire to control much of the Western world before he was destroyed.

Gullibility can also be used on a smaller scale such as when a child twists a parent around his/her little finger to get a toy in a store. No matter what the scale, the gullibility of others has been exploited and will continue to be as long as people are not aware of how their own weaknesses are used against them by manipulators.

What is Gullibility?

Gullibility means being easily cheated or tricked. Gullible people allow their boundaries to be invaded and accept others' reality as their own. There is so much garbage allowed in from the exterior that an individual's inner truth is suffocated. One of the most often used statements by people who have realized that they have been gullible is, "How could I have been so stupid?" No one likes to be taken in or tricked by anyone else, but without access to internal truth, the gullible person may be doomed to repeat the pattern many times. As if walking through a thick fog, gullible people are blind to seeing the part they play to create their own gullibility.

Confusing Gullibility with Innocence

Innocence is freedom from guile or cunning; it is simplicity. It implies purity, a trusting nature, not being tainted with a cynical attitude. Innocence is what many gullible people think that they are being. Images of the "innocence of a child" seem appealing because they imply a pristine quality of not yet having been jaded or armored with mistrust of the world. But innocence is different than gullibility in that inner truth is easily accessed when innocence is present. There is simplicity in the connection between the inner and outer world. To see this all we have to do is listen to a child quickly cut through the untruth. This is what the story, "Emperor's New Clothes" was about. The adults were willing to buy into the emperor's reality (mask's lie) that he was wearing clothes. It was the child who had the courage to speak the simple truth, "He has no clothes."

Manipulation as a Substitute for Self-responsibility

Manipulation means to manage or control artfully, by shrewd use of influence, often in an unfair or fraudulent way. *Manipulation is what bullies do* to hurt, frighten, or tyrannize people. Underlying manipulation is an internal desire to *get* something. Manipulation comes from a need to have others do something, be a certain way, or give something.

When we were young, we manipulated to get our needs met. For many of us it was a tool we used for our survival. But as adults, we no longer need to manipulate others to survive. We are completely self contained in our ability to meet our own needs and desires. If we manipulate now, we are doing it because at some level we have abdicated our responsibility to ourselves.

Gullibility and Manipulation as Opposite Sides of the Same Coin

Gullibility is to victimization as manipulation is to bullying. Both gullibility and manipulation are what is done to get others to take care of our needs and desires. So, like bullying and victimization, gullibility and manipulation are opposite sides of the same coin. Both the gullible one and the manipulator toss their self-responsibility back and forth in hopes that the other one will do what they are not willing to do for themselves.

Behind our mask of gullibility we are subject to manipulation because we are acting disconnected from our truth and power. Without tapping into our true power, we attach power and responsibility to others. Without listening to our truth, we have no way to check the validity and honesty of others' words and actions.

Rarely are we purely the gullible one or purely the manipulative one. We may frequently switch roles, sometimes in the middle of a situation. It is also important to remember, as we discussed in the sections on bullies and victims, that the *behavior* of people may seem gullible or manipulative, but the *real people* beneath are never either. Removing the mask of gullibility gets rid of our victimization. Removing the mask of manipulation gets rid of our bullying. Once these masks are off, our truth will feel safe enough to reveal itself to us.

Understanding the Difference Between Manipulation and Facilitation

To facilitate is to make easy or easier. Facilitation is the opposite of manipulation in that it comes from an internal desire to *give*. Facilitators are like wells which are fed by springs. They have no need to be filled up by someone else because they are filled from an internal source. There is no need to make others do or be any particular way.

Sometimes there is confusion about whether something is manipulation or facilitation. People who bully will cloak manipulation in the guise of facilitation in such statements as, "I'm only doing this for your own good." or "I am just trying to help you."

If you look at the underlying motives of statements such as these, manipulation is actually at the root. When a parent hits a child, saying it is to "discipline" the child, the hitting is really based on the parent's anger, frustration, or need to control. The parent is trying to get the child to do what the parent won't do for him or herself, which is to be self-disciplined. When friends give us unsolicited advice saying they want to help us, they really may want to live vicariously through us because they are not willing to take responsibility for their own lives.

A way to determine which is occurring, manipulation or facilitation, is to do this check: When someone is acting from their weakness or gullibility, what do we do? If we manipulate, we take advantage of the weakness or gullibility to turn it to our advantage. If we facilitate, we don't take advantage of the situation. Facilitators honor others boundaries and do not step on them, even when others invite them to.

Facilitators do not want anything in return from others except the pure joy of watching people open to their own truth. There is no need for recognition, thanks, or control. Facilitators do not *need* these outside things because they are already giving to themselves.

Controlling Groups Through Their Gullibility

People who have worn tyrant's masks through history have gotten special attention because of their ability to bully masses of people at the same time. They are held in reverence even though they are despised for their deeds. Much of the fascination with tyrants is how they could steam roll over so many people without being stopped.

There have been many books written about how particular tyrants, like Alexander the Great, Attila the Hun, Napoleon, and Hitler, were able to do what they did. But as a whole world civilization, we still haven't learned the lesson of tyranny. **The bullying behavior of tyrants is only considered powerful because people choose to be victims.** The many choose to cringe before the few or one, buying into the bullying contract that is held out to them.

How Groups are Manipulated

Not all methods of mass manipulation are as flamboyant and noteworthy as the tyrants mentioned above. But the principal ways of bullying groups of people through manipulation still applies whatever the level of tyranny. Whether the person acting like a tyrant is Saddam Hussein, a hijacker of an airline, a high school principal, a corporate boss, or an abusive parent, the methods used to bully groups of people are very similar.

Lumping people together to deny personal identity

One of the first things tyrants attempt to do is to strip away personal identity. Individuality is strictly taboo in a tyrannical system. Individuals are difficult to control because they have their own agenda, not the agenda of the tyrant.

So, herding people together like sheep is what any tyrants worth their salt will do. There are many ways to do this, but one of the best is to give all people the same new identity. Nationalism, slogans, flags, colors, special names, uniforms, mascots, lapel pens, and talking about the "team concept" all are ways to create a new identity.

People are willing to be victimized by tyrants when they become gullible. They suspend their own identities. These are the people who don't like their own identities anyway. They willingly give up the old with the hope that the new identities given by the tyrant will be better.

Grouping together in a herd is seen by most people as a way to connect to others. But what usually happens is that their connection ends up being more to the group itself rather than to the people in the group.

Keeping individuals moving and doing
If people are kept busy moving and doing, they will not have the time or energy left to think about what they personally want or need. They may feel frustrated, but since they are moving to the pace of the tyrant rather than their own, they may not even realize why they are frustrated.

Promoting the big lie
The lies may start out small as a test to see if tyrants will be challenged. When fabrications are not pointed out by others, the lies get bigger. Then the lies become outrageous. But by that time tyrants have people caught in their web of deceit like spiders drawing in their prey. People so want to believe what they are told that this way of deceiving groups works surprisingly well. The axiom of tyrants is: **Say the opposite of the truth with a straight face long enough and people will start to believe the lie.**

Diverting attention and energy away from the real issue
This is one of the oldest tricks in the tyrant's book. It is like telling people to look the other way while you steal something from them. But groups keep falling for it, so tyrants keep doing it.

They do this by:
1. Focusing energy on materialism and away from the inner longing for meaningful connections.

2. Focusing energy on production and away from individual's definition of self worth.

3. Developing a "common" enemy to keep people from seeing how they are being manipulated, used, or lied to by the organization and tyrant.

4. Playing groups against one another so they channel anger away from the organization and the tyrant.

Keeping people ignorant so they won't see the whole story

Doling out small pieces of information without giving away the whole picture is a very common ploy used by the tyrant to control groups of people. If people don't know the real story, they generally will not be angry.

Just to throw groups off the scent, tyrants will sometimes give out "disinformation" (lies) when a few people get close to discovering what is really going on. Tyrants hope to divert the group attention to chasing down false trails so the real story can remain hidden.

Exploiting individual's weaknesses

The hallmark of all good tyrants is to manipulate groups by exploiting individual weaknesses. When people feel weak or inadequate in a personal area, they are easy targets for conversion to an organization's cause.

Here are some of the ways weaknesses are used to

further the tyrant's organizational cause:*

Individual Weaknesses	Through Group Manipulation Become
•Sense of isolation	•Group belonging
•Low self worth	•Being a somebody in the organization
•Personal poverty	•Social status bestowed by manipulator
•Lost faith in self	•Faith in the cause
•Feel personal business is boring	•Spying on others, spreading gossip
•No sense of personal excellence	•Proclaim excellence for cause

Why Individuals Accept Group Manipulation

Tyrants delude themselves and those they victimize into believing that they can decide better for groups of people than individuals can decide for themselves. Responsibility is given over to the tyrant, without question, by most who choose to be manipulated.

But why is it that so many individuals are willing to be bullied along with others? **Most people don't want the responsibility which comes**

---

* Eric Hoffer, *The True Believer* (New York: Harper and Row, Publishers, Inc., 1951), p. 12–16.

with freedom. Freedom requires that we accept responsibility for all that happens to us. And responsibility requires us to think and feel on our own. Most people are not willing to do that. It feels like a burden. We would much rather have others to blame when things do not go our way. And as we have seen earlier, this is the classic victim mentality.

If we see the world as a harsh or scary place to be, we may also seek others to take responsibility for us, because we feel that we need a cushion between us and the "big bad world." We place ourselves in the role of children who still need to be protected by parents. At some level we feel that we are too little to be out in the world on our own. It is as if we have our eyes tightly closed, so we won't have to see the scary things in the maze of life. We want someone, anyone, to lead us through the maze, so we can pretend we are not scared.

Those who manipulate groups of people play on the fact that individuals choose to relinquish personal responsibility in some fundamental areas. They exploit individuals by offering to take the responsibility. They promise to fulfill our needs and desires for us. They count on our wanting to remain children, with our eyes closed, so we won't be aware of what is being done to us. Here are a few of our issues exploited by those who manipulate us:

They play on our desire to make order out of chaos.

As human beings, we have a desire to bring meaning to our lives. We seek to make order out of the universe, which can feel very chaotic at times. We want to solve the universal puzzle, so we can find our place in it. And we want to tame the unpredictable so we can feel safe in the world around us.

In our desire to understand, we look for clues from others who are also searching for the same thing. We are served by others when we take pieces of information from them with a grain of salt and adopt only what fits internally. Then, we remain independent thinkers.

We become subject to the manipulation of others when we suspend our thinking and say to ourselves, "They have the *true* answers. I'll stop searching and follow them." It is following of others unquestioningly, that makes it easy for them to lead us around by the nose.

They play to our desire for connection.

Human beings need connection to other humans to thrive and fully enjoy life. As we become adults, it is important that we fully connect to ourselves at all levels, so we will be able to determine how much connection with others we really need. Otherwise, we begin to "cling" to others in a desperate attempt to have others fill that black hole within us that is our lack of self-connection.

When we substitute external for internal connection, we may seek to "belong." We begin to define ourselves by the groups of people we associate with. We do this if we define ourselves through our nationality, our social status, job title, political affiliation, etc. It is when we define ourselves in terms of others, that we are subject to group manipulation.

This is not to say that just because we are members of groups, we necessarily are subject to manipulation, or that we lack self-connection if we are in a group. But if our identity *depends* on the group, or if we care what they think of us, we are opening ourselves to group manipulation.

They play on our desire to contribute to the world.

We all have a desire to contribute to the world in some way. We want to make a difference and feel that the world has been changed because of our unique contribution. We want to feel that there is a "reason" for being here.

People who are not clear about their individual gifts to the world, or their reason for being here, may seek others to define their contribution for them. Instead of excellence being claimed internally, it is defined in terms of being a part of an "excellent organization." Then our fulfillment is defined in terms of what we give to the organization. The organization decides rather than us what is given to the rest of the world.

They play on our desire for immortality.
Part of our desire to contribute to the world is our desire to feel that a part of us lives on after the deterioration of our physical bodies. We want to leave something behind to show that we existed. We also want to feel linked with other generations to give us a sense that we are part of an eternal continuity.

When we feel confused or unclear about our own immortality issues, we may allow groups to tell us what we have to do to become immortal. Tyrants use promises of immortality as our reward for performing our tasks for the organization. "If you do this, you will be remembered." The implication is that if you don't do what they want, you will be forgotten.

They play on our desire to feel powerful.
We all have a desire to be a powerful human force in the world. We want to feel a sense of control over our own destiny.

Many people have felt so mashed down during their lives that they lose this sense of personal power. In an effort to regain it, they may look to others outside themselves who promise to give them that lost power.

The collective energy which we may feel by being part of a group can be a substitute for personal power (if we are not accessing our power independent of the group). Groups give us a sense of strength when we aren't willing to rely on our own strength. What we give up by relying on group strength is control over our own destiny. Now our destiny lies in the hands of the group.

They play on our desire to feel love.
We all have a desire to receive and give unconditional love. When we allow love to flow in and out unhampered, we are able to make straight line connections to others.

If we shut off the flow of love on either the incoming or the outgoing end, we numb out to our experience of life on some level. When we are in this numbed state, we are subject to tyrants' offering groups who will "love us."

The groups will gladly take us in and show us love, but they usually have conditions attached. The conditions are that we must show our loyalty to the group by doing things the way that they do, or perceive life their way. If we do not adhere to the conditions, the love is often cut off just as quickly as it was turned on, because it is not real love, it is manipulation.

They play on our faith in something greater than ourselves.
All of us have faith in something greater than ourselves. We can have faith in human nature, faith in God, faith in the future, faith in a righteous cause. Whatever that faith is, it is something that connects us to a greater whole.

When we are not willing to honor or unclear about where our faith lies, we can be drawn like magnets into groups. We see the group energy as something greater than us. It can whip us into a fervor of belief in a cause, as a substitute for faith in ourselves and our ability to make a direct connection to the world.

The group also can serve as a buffer between us and whatever we perceive is greater. This happens most often when we feel very weak and perceive the "greater" as overwhelmingly powerful. We may feel that if we stood alone without the strength of the group, we would be annihilated or completely absorbed by the greater power.

They play on our desire for hope.
We all have a desire for our expectations in life to be fulfilled. We have "hope" that the future will be better, hope that there is life after death, hope that we will get a check in the mail, and so on.

Sometimes, because of repeated disappointments, we begin to lose hope that we can fulfill our own expectations. We begin to doubt ourselves. This is when we are most likely to place our hope in groups.

Tyrants use groups to channel everyone's hopes in one direction. Any deviation from the group hope is seen as subversion and sabotage. Sometimes groups are convinced to shun or pity those who do not share the group hope. All of these tactics are designed to manipulate groups into focusing energy in the direction the tyrant wants the energy to go, instead of the way that each person would naturally be guided.

They play on our desire for freedom.
Our essence desires to be free. We all know this at a deep level. We want to be free of the oppression and pressure which is placed on us.

But many of us still believe the portion of the "mask's lying contract" which states that self-responsibility is an oppressive responsibility. Never having been truly self-responsible, we do not understand the freedom which comes from self-responsibility. So we fear freedom more than we do the oppression of the mask.

Tyrants know that we fear self-responsibility, so they offer us an alternative to freedom through groups. **What they offer us is parental care in exchange for our adult freedom.** When we are part of a group, we no longer have to make decisions. Decisions are made for us and given to us as rules to follow. We no longer have to think for ourselves. The thinking is done for us and handed back to us as doctrine. We no longer have to feel our own feelings. Emotions are sanitized for us and come back to us as "fervor for the cause." We no longer have to be responsible for our actions. Actions are translated for us and handed back as orders which must be followed.

They play on our desire for truth.
Our desire for truth is a fundamental part of our human nature. To find truth is to find ourselves. The truth is our foundation. When we build our lives on our truth, we know that our individuality is

solid. We can withstand whatever is encountered in life.

If we are not connected to our truth, our lives are built on shaky foundations. In our desperation to keep our lives from crumbling, we may look outside ourselves to find truth. When we are offered a group truth to cling to, we may grab onto it as a means of survival.

We fall prey to group manipulation when we believe that our truth must exactly coincide with the group's truth. Tyrants are great promoters of "the one truth" which is, of course, their own. Good tyrants are able to convince groups that "the one truth" will solve the problems of the world, sometime in the future. Not now, of course, but if followed over a period of time, people's lives will be changed. But when we build our lives on *anyone else's truth*, our lives are never really our own.

By following truths outside ourselves, we buy the underlying implication that we can "escape" what we don't like about ourselves.

> "The urge to escape our real self is also an urge to escape the rational and the obvious. The refusal to see ourselves as we are develops a distaste for facts and cold logic."**

** Eric Hoffer, *The True Believer* (New York: Harper and Row, Publishers, Inc., 1951), p. 83.

To believe the truth of groups, we must "unbelieve" everything else that does not fit the group belief. When new information is encountered, instead of opening ourselves to see if it has validity for our individual truth, we throw it out as not relevant to "the belief."

Tyrants know this group dynamic. Once they have you as a group "insider," they are able to step up the manipulation and get groups to do what no individual would do without the support of others.

Pretending Others Can Think for Us

Of course, no one can ever really do the thinking for us. Even when tyrants offer and groups accept, the contract can never really be fulfilled. Since we are all unique individuals, even when we relinquish our responsibility and turn our thinking over to others, we eventually become discontent, angry, rebellious, or deadened.

So we accept the tyrant masks' version of the Game of "Let's Pretend." The variation that we play to be manipulated in groups is "The Sheep that Graze Together, Stay in a Daze Together."

Making Ourselves
Easy Prey to Manipulation

To those who manipulate, our being gullible is like wearing a sign around our necks saying, "Take me, I'm yours. Have your way with me."

114

MANIPULATION AND GULLIBILITY

Manipulators see the signs we wear even when we are unaware of wearing them. They are good at reading people. They scan us and take our measure. They scrutinize us to see if we are willing to be controlled or exploited. It is as if they have invisible hooks out to see where we can be snagged like unsuspecting minnows.

There is a childlike glee sparked in people who manipulate when they are able to draw us onto their hooks of control. When we don't take their bait, they quickly lose interest in us and move on to more fertile waters. There will be others who are more easily hooked, for there are plenty of other people wearing gullibility signs.

Why is it that we allow ourselves to be manipulated? What makes us such easy prey? And what is it about us that allows manipulators to read our gullibility sign so clearly?

They play on our lack of self-understanding.

Any time we feel that we need to justify our feelings or thoughts to anyone, we are setting ourselves up for exploitation. The only reason we will feel that we need to justify ourselves is that we don't know who we are.

People who ask us to justify ourselves are doing so because they are trying to relieve the pressure on themselves due to their own lack of self-understanding. They are generally doing one of two things. They may be attempting to focus the pressure on us so that we will not notice their own lack of

115

self-understanding. Or they may have the same lack self-understanding that we do. They hope that we will explain things to them so they don't have to figure things out for themselves.

They play on our willingness to do self-condemnation.

If we do self-condemnation, we are like walking targets for others to throw condemnation our way. People who have an abundance of their own self-condemnation are carrying so much of it that they are just looking for others to shame so they can relieve some of the burden. They believe that by shaming us they will somehow feel less shame themselves. Of course, shaming others usually has the opposite effect. It simply adds to the burden of self-condemnation.

They play on our feeling that something is missing.

When we feel like something is missing inside, we will try to get others to fill us up. For anyone wearing a bullying mask, this is a golden opportunity to exploit us for their own purposes.

They will promise to give us what we are missing in exchange for our giving ourselves over to their control. If we take the bait, they can feel superior to us. Since they can never really give us what we are missing, we will feel shafted and used. We may feel afraid of never really getting filled up, which makes us ripe for the plucking all over again.

They play on our being scared of being hurt.
If we are scared of being hurt, our whole being will radiate that just like a light in the night attracting bugs. We will attract people wearing bully masks disguised as people who will protect us from being hurt. All that these exploiters will do, is to comfort us with one hand and hurt us with the other.

They will do this because they are afraid of being hurt themselves. If they can keep us at a distance by hurting us as well as comforting us, they are not as afraid that we will get close enough to hurt them or expose them for who are afraid they are.

They play on our caring about how others perceive us.
If we care about what others think of us, we will attract exploiters who are disguised as our friends. They will offer to tell us what we want to hear. In exchange, we will have to do what they want us to do or be who they want us to be.

If we decide later we no longer want to do their bidding, they will shame us and attempt to make us feel isolated or a misfit, not worthy of others' notice. If these exploiters have issues about how others perceive them, they may feel a lot of shame that we no longer perceive them the way they want us to.

THE LIES OF THE MASK

Ways We Let Manipulators Toy with Our Reality

As we discussed earlier, to believe that the "mask's lying contract" has any hold over us, we must sacrifice our reality and believe the reality of those who manipulate us. Here are some of the ways we do that:

We trust words told to us and ignore all other signs.

Spoken words are only a small part of the total communication which goes on between people. There are many other signs which indicate what people are truly saying. A few of the other important signs are: tone, inflection, volume, body language, and demeanor. There is also energy radiated by others which can give us information about their truth. This is what is being felt when we say someone has "good vibes."

First impressions can be extremely helpful. For those who are prone to gullibility, this may be vital information. The impression we form before our programming takes over can give us a momentary clear "window of understanding" about others before we cloud over our knowingness with outside data.

We only hear what we want to believe and disregard the rest.

We may so want to believe others that even when they tell exactly how they will manipulate us, we ignore it. We listen only to the surface statements of

118

praise and promise. We filter out slams against us and cutting remarks. And we totally block out lies or statements about how others have also been similarly manipulated.

We don't read between the lines to get underlying messages.

Manipulators may test us to see if we are gullible by playing the game of "fill in the gap." They will give us clues that we are being manipulated without giving us all of the pieces. Then, they pay attention to see if we are onto their game by noticing whether we fill in the missing pieces of the puzzle.

Sometimes the game is played by giving individual statements which are true, but create an overall false impression. We are tested to see if we are sucked into the falsity. In another variation of the game, important information is omitted which creates a false picture. We are tested to see if we can figure out what information is missing.

If we figure out the game and let manipulators know we are on to them, they will likely stop playing with us. Much of the fun of the game is lost when their tricks are revealed. They feel uncomfortable when their deception is exposed.

We don't scrutinize the truth of what is said.

Manipulators will check to see if we call them on the lie or ask for verification of the truth. If we don't challenge them, they will go for a bigger lie to see if we will buy it. This cycle continues until we are totally under their control, or we stop them and say "No more lies."

We feel bound to bargains no matter how circumstances change.

If we feel we need to be conscientious toward others no matter what the cost to ourselves, we are ripe for manipulator's pickings. We may find others lying to us, or not disclosing the total picture but expecting us to adhere to our end of the agreement. Manipulators will say, "You promised. Now you are stuck." If we feel guilty or act like they are right, we are asking to be taken.

We believe what others tell us about ourselves and our situation.

When we don't know ourselves, we look for others to tell us what we are like. Manipulators jump at this chance because they know that we are at our most malleable state in our "not knowingness." They can mold us into who they want us to be for their own purposes.

We can also be manipulated in much the same way when we have not assessed our own situation. If we ask others to do the assessment, chances are they will manipulate the facts to suit their own purposes. They will attempt to bleed off all of our assets and leave us with only our liabilities.

We give greater weight to the written word than is deserved.

Just because something is in writing does not mean that we should give it any more credibility than if it is spoken. Some gullible people have a tendency to believe that if it is written down, it is like the Ten Commandments handed down from Mount Sinai. Actually, lies, misleading statements, or other information intended to manipulate can be as easily put on paper. It doesn't just come out of people's mouths. Just because something is written down does not mean it deserves to be believed.

We defer to others' perceived expertise or authority.

As gullible people, we may trust what others say or do because we believe they have more power or special knowledge in a certain field than we do. Our trust may go well beyond the level of trust they deserve. Instead of trusting our perception of the situation, we defer to their perceived status. We don't challenge outrageous activities of "experts" and "authority figures" because we don't believe that our perceptions have equal validity with theirs.

We don't connect our intuition to our reasoning.

If our intuition and reasoning are not wired together, we are likely to be easy targets for manipulators. When we operate strictly from one or the other, we are handicapped.

When we only use reason without intuition, we will likely be hooked by manipulators in endless "logical" justification to do things their way. Eventually they will be able to find just the right hole in our logic to back us into a corner, so we feel trapped in their control.

If we operate only from intuition without including our ability to reason, we can get swept up emotionally into the excitement of the moment. We may believe the promise, without thinking clearly enough to realize that it makes no sense.

Ways We Let Manipulators Toy with Our Trust

We all want to be trusting people, but as gullible people there are ways that we do not *trust wisely*. Here are some ways we sacrifice our wisdom regarding who to trust:

We show our soft underbelly before natural levels of trust are built.

Gullible people often do not respect their own boundaries and unwittingly invite manipulators in to mess with their psyche. Trust takes time to develop because it needs to *not only be believed but demonstrated as well.* Gullible people do not give trust time to grow, they want immediate trust. When manipulators see this desire, they seize on it as a golden opportunity. They use gullible people's trust to tighten the screws of their grip.

We believe others motives are pure.
As gullible people we may assume that others have pure motives. But rarely are anyone's motives completely pure because so many of us wear masks. Our motives may be a mixture of good intentions and manipulations without our being consciously aware of it.

Manipulators may purposely or inadvertently hide their motives from us. Asking questions can give us more details to clarify whether manipulation is mixed in with their good intentions. They may not be truthful in the answers, but as we develop the ability to read people, we begin to see the truth of their motives in spite of their verbal statements.

Ways We Let Manipulators Toy with Our Emotions

Buying into the "mask's lying contract" means that we have agreed to deny our emotions in favor of what others choose for us to feel. Here are some of the ways we allow our emotions to play directly into the hands of manipulators:

We want to avoid conflict.
If we feel that we need to keep the peace at all costs, we will likely sacrifice ourselves to manipulators at some point in our lives. Manipulators will fan the flames of conflict to see if we can be smoked out of our position and collapse into their waiting, controlling arms.

THE LIES OF THE MASK

We are afraid of anger.
When we are afraid of others' rage, manipulators will get angry with us. They may scream, yell, or throw things to control us. They will watch us dart around like scared rabbits attempting to find hiding places. When we feel desperate for a place of shelter, manipulators will step in to offer us refuge under their protective but smothering wings.

We let our "bleeding hearts" rule decisions.
Manipulators see our compassion for others as weakness and will seize on the opportunity to use it against us. They attempt to make gullible people take responsibility for others' hurts or mistakes. Manipulators will give us some sob story about why they need help and will act as though *we* are the only ones who can correct the injustices done to them.

There is a great "Far Side" cartoon by Gary Larson which illustrates the absurdity of a person's bleeding heart gullibility. In it are two women standing at a door. One is about to open the door. In the window next to the door we see a giant bug the size of the women. One woman turns to the other and says, "Calm down, Edna. Yes, it's some giant, hideous insect...but it could be some giant, hideous insect in need of help."*** If we take the "bleeding heart" bait without analyzing whether *we will hurt*

*** Gary Larson, *The Far Side Calendar 1991* (Kansas City: Universal Press Syndicate, 1990), Sunday, September 29.

ourselves by helping others, we are just the suckers manipulators are looking for.

Ways We Let Manipulators Toy with Our Good Nature

In our effort to deny that we have any bad feelings about ourselves, we may begin to play the role, of the "good" one. When we attempt to hold onto this role we allow manipulators to take advantage of us because they know we don't want to appear the least bit "bad." Here are some of the ways we allow ourselves to let manipulators twist us around their little finger:

We don't want to seem impolite.

As gullible people we may have been raised with the belief that we must be polite, no matter what the personal cost. If we believe this we lay ourselves wide open to manipulation.

Manipulators may run a "politeness check" on us to see how tenaciously we will hold onto our need to be nice, sweet, gracious, or generous. They may become rude or impolite to get our reaction. If we become nicer when they become rude, they know they can push us around.

We mistake passivity for peacefulness.

Many of us have allowed ourselves to be mashed down through years of being pounded on by others. We have become very passive in our responses to the outside world.

We sometimes may confuse this passivity for being internally peaceful. Actually our doormat-like behavior only indicates that we are numb to life, not peaceful. Peaceful people radiate out their energy. They give the message to the outside world, "Turbulence is not welcome here. Try somewhere else." Doormats invite in the turbulence with lettering which says, "Welcome. Wipe your feet here."

We let others dump on us.

If we act like the city dump, we may attract large gatherings of people (not to mention flies). Manipulators are always looking for a good scapegoat, so gullible people should be prepared for an onslaught of attention. If we are willing to take on others' garbage, many will oblige us by heaping it on us. The more we are willing to take, the more it will be piled on. Only we can decide when the dumping ends.

We put others' needs and desires above ours.

If we put others' needs and desires above ours, we invite manipulators to abuse our giving nature. Others see self-sacrifice as a stupid thing to do since they put themselves first. Their attitude may be, "Okay, you asked for it. I'll help you be last on your list if you insist."

We mistake manipulation for assertiveness.

When we are gullible we may mistake manipulation for assertiveness. We don't challenge manipulators because we believe that they are "learning how to be an adult," or "expressing themselves." What we ignore is the fact that they are stepping on us to be who they are. When we do not stop the behavior, we teach others that its okay to become a bully and use manipulative tactics to get what is wanted.

We would rather be gullible than manipulate others.

Sometimes we don't see other options besides gullibility and manipulation. Since we know how it hurts to be manipulated, we would rather hurt ourselves by remaining gullible than be the one hurting others through manipulation.

Ways We Let Manipulators Treat Us Like Children

As we have seen already, many adults are really children except in physical form. When we act like children, we are inviting manipulators to treat us like children. Here are some ways we do that:

We want to believe the unbelievable.

The childlike part of us wants to believe that others have magic which we don't have. We want to believe that they are able to do for us what we are not willing to do for ourselves. So we suspend our belief system to temporarily incorporate something improbable.

If we understand that we are playing the game of "make believe" we can have fun. But if we take the game seriously, we set ourselves up for manipulation. Gullible people do not want to believe what is usually the case, "If it sounds too good to be true, it probably is." We will remain gullible as long as we still seriously look outside ourselves for "pie in the sky."

We want easy answers.

Most of us would like the answers to our questions and problems in life to be easy. Manipulators know that we want problems to go away. They know that we don't want to unravel complexities in our lives. They also know that most of us don't want to spend the energy it would take to figure things out.

Manipulators will gladly step in and tell us that they have the answers for us. They want us to think that they can take care of everything so we won't have worry "our pretty little heads."

We want quick fixes.

Like easy answers, we want to believe in the quick fix. We don't want to take the time to deal with the details of our lives. We don't want to wait for time to take care of things. We are in a hurry and want what we want right now!

In our dash for the quick fix, we hand our treasures over to others on a silver tray. We hope that they will fix our treasures and give them right back. But what usually happens is that the manipulator decides to keep our treasures. When we get them back, they are picked clean and are of very little value to us anymore.

We want our future to be assured.
No one knows what the future holds for anyone. We may predict and look at likely odds, but anything we do is a guess, because the future is not in our human control.

If we are scared about what the future will bring to us, we are likely to believe others who promise to make our future secure. As gullible people we want to believe that the uncontrollable can be controlled. We will put our future in the hands of a manipulator rather than take our own chances.

We deny that we have opinions and adopt others' positions.
As gullible people we may act as if we do not have opinions. We ask what others think or feel. Then we judge what we think, feel or say based on those around us rather than on our own truth.

One of the gullibility tests that manipulators use is that of checking to see if we are willing to stand behind our opinions and positions. Or, are we willing to give ours up to believe in theirs. When we don't stand our ground, they know we live externally by our weakness and can be made to do what they want.

THE LIES OF THE MASK

We act like we have limited options.
As gullible people we believe that we have limited options. This sets us up for manipulation by others offering to expand the options for us.

Just when we are hooked into the belief that manipulators will expand our choices, they pretend to clamp the hand irons on us and chain us to the wall. They attempt to make us believe that they have us at their mercy. They show us the portion of the "mask's lying contract" which says that the contract is binding. They insist that we have no other choice but to do as they say. If we believe them, we remain trapped in their imaginary game.

We confuse control and manipulation for love and support.
Gullible people are usually people who fear loss of approval and support from others. Part of our gullibility is believing that we cannot get what we really want, so we must cling to what others are willing to dole out to us.

That belief radiates out an energy to others that says, "I don't deserve more than this." Manipulators know that our low deserve level means that we will grovel at their feet for whatever small pittance they choose to give us. They know that they can offer us an inferior substitute for what we really want, because we will not ask for more.

We believe we must do what we are told to do.

As gullible people we may have had obedience so ingrained into us that we now operate without thinking, taking orders from anyone giving them. We listen more carefully to what manipulators tell us than we listen to ourselves. This is because we are programmed to listen to outside commands and to suppress any internal directives.

We are rewarded for our gullibility.

As gullible people we may have a long history of being rewarded for our passivity or playing victim. In this victim stance, we settle for a pat on the head from someone who says, "There...There...You are so good, understanding, patient, etc." We act more like dogs than human beings. We wait for our "master, the manipulator" to feed us and throw us treats instead of going for life on our own.

We are not willing to take adult responsibility for our lives.

As gullible people we feel that it is much easier to have others to blame for our gullibility than to take responsibility for our own lives. We may be just comfortable enough in our lives the way they are that we are complacent about taking responsibility. We may think that if we can just get others to change, that we won't have to wade through our own mess. We may feel that we are not strong enough or have the courage to take self-responsibility. Whatever the reason for ducking our responsibility to ourselves,

131

when we toss it outside us, we immediately hang our gullibility sign out for others to see.

Ending the Pretense

To stop the "games of the mask" requires that we end the pretense. We must be willing to examine ourselves for who we truly are. We have to take responsibility for all aspects of our lives. And we must be willing to love the people underneath our own masks and live from our truth. **Once we are living from our truth, the mask can no longer make us do or be anything against our wishes.** The power it once had will evaporate because we are no longer willing to accept the "mask's lying contract" or fall prey to the manipulation of ourselves or others.

Part 3

Shedding the
Layers of the Mask

CHAPTER 8
Releasing the Tight Grip of the Mask

"Is it safe to come out, now? I think I'm ready."

Removing the mask is both a goal and a process in our effort to live from our truth. But to expect that we will just be able to take off the mask all at once may be unrealistic. Since we have had so long to pile layer upon layer of varnish on the mask we have created, it may be difficult to remove.

If we become impatient with our ability to remove the mask, we will actually slow down the process. We are only able to shed layers of the mask when they are ready to come off and not before. It is like getting a skinned knee. The skin forms a scab to protect the wound. When it is ready, the scab sloughs off naturally. The wound must have its own time to heal. If we get in a hurry to get rid of the scab and pick at it, we may damage the tender new skin beneath and slow down the healing process.

We need to allow ourselves time to slough off the mask naturally. As we become gentler with ourselves and closer to living from our truth, we will understand that this is what we must do to be free of the mask.

Benefits from Showing Our Face

The world will give us lots of reasons for keeping our mask on. But let's examine some of the reasons to go against our conditioning and take it off.

To reconnect with the world

As human beings, we all deeply desire connection to others. We want to be loved for who we are. But wearing the mask keeps us from truly touching others. We become like the "bubble boy" living inside a cocoon. We may be insulated from the germs, (or hurt), but we also can never experience the powerful healing energy of touch from another human being. Our cocoon becomes our prison. Removing the mask and showing our face, allows us to really make contact with the world.

To breathe fully and feel safe in our bodies

With the mask on, life starts to feel smothering. The thicker the mask we have created for ourselves, the more difficult it becomes to breathe. We begin to concentrate our energy on just breathing to stay alive.

As our breathing becomes more labored and shallow, we cut off the flow of blood to our extremities. We start to lose feeling in our hands and feet. And when our feet can't feel the ground, we start to become panicky. We must have solid contact with the earth to feel safe.

When we begin to feel unsafe, we contract our life energy inward in a survival mode. Our gut tenses up as energy becomes concentrated in fight or flight mode. Removing the mask helps us to breath again and feel safer in our bodies and in the world.

To recover our sensations and feel fully alive
With our mask on, our senses become dulled. Colors are not as vivid. Sounds are not as clear. Tastes are flatter, and smells may become indistinguishable from one another. The senses become dulled gradually so that over time, we do not realize that our world has become almost two-dimensional. We begin to miss out on life's joy and excitement. Showing our face helps us to feel alive again and ready to partake of all that life has to offer. We are able to recover the wonder and awe which we once had as children.

To remember simplicity
Great teachers and masters have each discovered for themselves the simplicity of life. This is why their messages have been simple. But knowing this is not just reserved for the great masters of the world.

As our faces begin to come into clear focus, we will also see that there is great simplicity at our core. We will remember that we knew this as children. We will rediscover that the essence has always been simple. What we put on top of it to keep it down is what we call complex.

So it is also with truth. It is simple and straightforward. It is the lies we manufacture to cover the truth which become twisted, distorted, and convoluted.

Acknowledging this simplicity can give great freedom. The complication we create in our lives by playing the games and wearing masks is part of the mask's lie. Just knowing this helps us to begin to end the lies and proudly show our face for all to see.

To feel lighter

We can start to feel very heavy in our masks. Especially if we have spent many years slapping new layers of glop on the surface of it. We may feel like we are carrying a great burden which weighs us down. Our shoulders start to sag under the load. Our backs hurt. With all the extra pounds we haul around, we feel lethargic. Every step is taken with great effort. Removing the mask can feel like we have punched through a thick paper maché shell. We throw off the burdens. We may feel so light that we will need to check to see if we are still standing on the ground.

To recover our full range of emotions

When we are hiding behind our mask, it is difficult to allow our face to truly have emotions of its own. Our face has become molded into the fixed position of the mask. Since we are playing a role, we have to stay within the role even when we really feel something else. Removing the mask allows us to quit suppressing the real feelings we have, so we can regain our full range of emotions.

SHEDDING THE LAYERS OF THE MASK

To stop the inner war
Living from behind a mask means that we carry
on an internal war between the inner and the outer
self. It is difficult to ever feel like we can rest, when
we are on constant battle alert.
A lot of energy has to go into creating a fight or
flight atmosphere internally for the war effort. Our
mind has to be ready with alternate strategies for
how best to attack or defend. Our emotions have to
be on guard to protect us when we call out for them.
And our bodies have to pump lots of adrenalin to the
entire system so that we can be ready to march
forward, or retreat at a moment's notice.
Ending the inner war means we can calm down
and rest. We can put our lives back together the way
we choose, rather than marching to someone else's
orders.

To find our natural pace
Once we have been able to stop the inner war
which has gone on due to hiding behind a mask, we
can begin to find our own pace for living.
The mask may have told us to hurry all of the
time. We may feel like we have been running an
endless race to nowhere. The mask may have told us
to slow down and been holding us back, like a dog on
a leash. Whatever the pace, the one the mask set for
us is almost undoubtedly one which doesn't fit for us,
because it was assigned to us, rather than our own.
Since each person has their own rhythm, freeing

ourselves from the mask will allow us to see how we choose to face the world and at what pace.

To laugh again and experience the joy of life
Sometimes the drama of the mask can appear to be a tragedy, full of dark sadness. Once we start focusing on the tragedy, we start to see life through tragic eyes. We may forget that life has a lighter side, too. Situations and people can be pretty funny at times. When we have our face free of the mask, we can start to wipe away the tears and laugh fully again without feeling constrained. Removing the mask also helps us to see that joy can be found, if we start to see life through joyful eyes.

To allow us to see the patterns in our life
We get caught up in the role we are playing while in the mask. When our energy is consumed in this way, we have a difficult time stepping out of the role to see ourselves in the bigger picture of life. It is from the broader viewpoint that we are able to get a better perspective on our part in the dramatic game we have created. Removing the mask helps us to see things in a way which can give us insight about ourselves and those around us.

To sense our REAL power
Behind the mask, there is no way our true power can exert itself. It is imprisoned behind a barbed wire barricade. So in our mask, we create the illusion of power. We may puff our mask up like a blowfish to look bigger than we really are to would-

be predators. We may put on a layer of "monster" makeup over the existing mask to scare people away. Whatever we do to feel powerful in our mask always fails because the only real power we have is underneath the mask. Removing the mask allows our true power to assert itself. Because it comes from the real us, our true power is not invasive of others. It is clean and pure, assisting us to simply take up the space we naturally have in the world.

To fulfill our deepest desires
It is difficult to fulfill our deepest desires when we are wearing a mask. There is so much energy spent on playing the role that there is no time left to do what we really want to do. Wearing the mask conditions us to doing things with our time that we feel we "should" do to keep in character with the mask. The mask with all its outside programming will tell us that our deepest desires are unwise, unhealthy, impractical, expensive, or impossible. Removing the mask, and revealing our face, allows us to listen to ourselves so we know that our desires are not only possible, but are what we are meant to do.

To have freedom to be whoever we choose
Since the mask sits rigidly on our face, it can never really fit. No matter how much we adjust it to be compatible with our face, it constricts us. The field of vision within the mask, therefore, is narrow. The illusion is created that there are limited patterns of being in the world. Removing the mask helps us

get rid of this irritating facade, which never did fit us anyway. We begin to see that our choices are unlimited. We are free to be whoever we choose. Just as we once chose the mask we wear, we can now choose to take it off and be the free spirit we were meant to be.

Interwoven Emotions, Mind, and Body as Clues to Our Truth

Our body, mind and emotions are integrally linked creating the wholeness which is our internal universe. When we are out of balance in one of these three areas, it causes stress to the other parts.

We get clues from our body, mind, and emotions which help us understand ourselves and the world. Once we are aware that these clues are a natural part of our self-discovery process, we are able to open ourselves to the messages each part gives.

Some people mistake the clues for flaws. When we view ourselves as flawed, then we may turn against ourselves and deny ourselves the very help that our clues are attempting to give us. Unmasking the messages of the body, emotions and thoughts for what they really are is one of the major keys to the recovery of our truth and connection to our essence.

The gift of emotions

Emotions come from having feelings aroused to the point of awareness. Emotions give texture to our lives. They bring pure consciousness into the body to be experienced. Without emotions we wouldn't experience laughter, crying, dancing, and singing.

But part of the mask's lying contract is that only the mask decides what emotions are permitted. So the mask we wear encourages us to shut off certain emotions, or bury our emotions under one another. If we deny any of our emotions, we get out of balance and make it more likely that we will become bullies or victims. Denial focuses so much energy into keeping emotions hidden that it is like trying to hide a barking dog from our landlord neighbor. We can muzzle it for a while, but eventually it cannot be contained and must let out the barks or die.

What is required is diving into our emotions and feeling fully whatever emotions are there. This is how we get the maximum benefit from the gift of our emotions. Fully feeling all of our emotions restores our passion which enhances our experiences. Living with passion versus living without, is like the difference between living a holographic life, instead of a snapshot.

Diving fully into our emotions does not mean that we unload our emotions indiscriminately. It does means that we explore what messages our emotions are telling us. This may mean going more deeply within ourselves than we have ever gone before. When we allow our body and mind to assist us, we are able to more safely go to greater depths within because our emotions know that all of us is willing to finally listen to the message.

RELEASING THE TIGHT GRIP OF THE MASK

The power of the mind

The mind is a storehouse of information. But it is much more than that. Our thoughts also give us a context for expansion and new understanding of ourselves and the universe we live in. Without our thoughts to guide us we would have no reference points. Without reference points we would not know who we are or see ourselves as having unique gifts to give to the world.

The body and emotions have clues for us, but without the reasoning ability of the mind, the clues remain nebulous abstractions. It is the mind which brings meaning to what is felt and experienced.

The meaning which is assigned to body signs and emotional stimuli is solely interpreted by the mind. If the mind can assign one interpretation, it can just as easily assign another, if it chooses. So the mind holds the cards in many ways. Will it allow the messages from the body and emotions to really come through, or will it choose to have the clues remain hidden forever?

Thinking about an experience is not experiencing

All reality was first a thought. Someone had to think of the idea of checking accounts, religion, nuclear weapons, and light bulbs before they could become a reality. Once we think the ideas, the possibility for bringing them into reality exists.

But thinking of experience is not the same as the experience. It is a start, but if we stop there, it will be the difference between reading a book about a foreign country and actually going there. The thought is only a thought until we bring it through our emotions and body into experience.

The gift of body wisdom

The body possesses an innate wisdom which can be a good gauge for what is going on inside the real us. It has a natural way of cooperating with our essence to urge us to wholeness. In fact, the state of our physical body is a reflection of the well-being of the rest of us.*

The body gives us clues about our emotional, mental, and spiritual state as well as our physical well-being. Many people are becoming aware of the part that stress plays in our lives. Stress is generally a sign that we need to slow down. We are not paying attention to what our natural being really wants. But other things like a burn on our finger or bruises on our elbow can give us valuable insight into issues affecting other parts of us as well.**

It is essential when we start to do deep emotional, mental, or spiritual exploration to be in touch with

---

* Deepak Chopra has an excellent book and tape series on this topic. The book is, *Quantum Healing-Exploring the Frontiers of Mind/Body Medicine* (New York: Bantam Books, 1989) and the tape series, *Magical Mind, Magical Body* (Chicago: Nightingale Conant, 1990).

** For anyone not familiar with this concept, you may want to read Louise Hay's books, *Heal Your Body* (Santa Monica: Hay House, 1988) or *You Can Heal Your Life* (Santa Monica: Hay House, 1984).

our body. This is our vehicle for release of the traumas experienced on the emotional, mental, and spiritual levels. Our body has the ability to get rid of the stored-up negative energy through our pores, voice, nose, bladder, rectum, hands, feet, etc. All we have to do is allow our body to do its natural job.

We are not our emotions, thoughts, or bodies
We are the feelers of the emotions, the thinker of the thoughts, and the designer of the body. We are our essence and that transcends all else. When we realize this very important fact, we allow our emotions, thoughts, and body freedom to do what they were meant to do. They are *tools* to be used to access our truth so we can live authentically.

Retrieving Our Individuality

What is discussed in this book is about being the individual we are capable of being. Removing the mask to reveal our face is only possible if we respect and *want* to retrieve our individuality. As we have seen, the mask attempts to make us believe that uniformity of thinking and being are a must. But, as we now understand, this is one of the biggest lies. The only hold the mask's lies have on us, is if we allow our individuality to be stifled. So freedom from the mask is freedom to be the independent people only we, individually, can be.

Feeling Raw at First

When we begin to shed layers of the mask, we may feel very raw and exposed to the outside world. This is a natural feeling as we are getting used to our essence living closer to the surface.

Rawness is the sensation which indicates our truth is more closely matching our outside reality, but is not yet used to being "out there." We may get messages from the mask that something is not right, that we should abandon the raw feeling. The mask always attempts to keep us from trying new feelings and ways of being, because it sees change as a threat.

If we are honest with ourselves, we realize the raw feeling is not really a bad feeling. It is only a new sensation we have not experienced before. There is a difference between rawness and pain, if we pay close attention. Recognizing the raw feeling for what it is allows us to become accustomed to the new sensation without shutting it off.

There may be a feeling that we need to pull the mask back on to protect us from feeling raw. If we do put the mask back on, while it may feel familiar, it will never again be as comfortable. We have now let our face breathe and feel life around it. Once it has had a taste of that freedom, it will never be satisfied with going back into total hiding.

Liking Who We See

As we begin shedding the layers of the mask, we begin to like more of who we see. We look at ourselves in the mirror and make contact with the real person. No longer will we feel like we are peeking through eye holes to get a glimpse of who we are.

Liking ourselves has a snowball effect. First we may feel in a momentary flash, "Hey, I'm not half bad." Then we may be able to say to ourselves, "I really love you. You are a wonderful human being." Later, we may be able to affirm to ourselves on a regular basis, "You are a great being meant to be here on this earth, just as you are." Eventually, we will have this knowledge about ourselves so ingrained that we will say the old affirmations and feel, "Of course. I *know* that."

Don't despair if it takes you time to love yourself and get to your truth. If you have had old recordings repeatedly telling you otherwise, it may take time to record over what has already been there for so long. Just know that the more that you love yourself, the more you love yourself. And the more you are truthful, the easier it becomes. This is not a selfish thing to do. It is a necessary foundation for you to be able to love others and give your special gifts to the world from your individual truth.

Understanding Comes
From Experience

What you read here, or any other place, will be totally irrelevant and meaningless unless you experience the truth of it for yourself. Understanding is not something which can be acquired by reading a lot of different books, or being educated in a certain way. It is not something that others can say to you and have you get.

Understanding only comes to us through experience. This is why so many ways of teaching fail. The people teaching and the person wanting to learn believe that something can be given to someone else and then they will know it. We can wish that we could open our heads and put the knowledge in. We may wish we could look at a book of music and know how to play the piano. But, that is not the way life works. It is through experience that we learn and develop understanding. We must practice life to experience it fully.

There is no prescribed order for shedding the layers of the mask to reveal your face. And there is no magic cure to be discussed in the rest of the book. What we will discuss are some of the most common issues which make us want to wear a mask. Just as creating the mask has been unique process for each of us, so is the way in which we shed it.

As you go through your process of self-discovery,

you may find other thoughts and techniques not mentioned here which are helpful. **Do not discount anything which works for you.** Be proud of your creativity. Be proud that you have experienced true self understanding and are rediscovering who you really are.

CHAPTER 9

Goodbye Bully, Goodbye Victim

"Goodbye old familiar buddy. It's time for me to experience life on my own."

One of the most challenging aspects of removing the mask is to get to the point of saying goodbye to the bully and victim roles we have played for so long. Without them, what do we do instead? How will we deal with others who still play these roles with us? And will we still be able to fit into society, or instead be misfits on the fringe when we say goodbye?

Only you can answer these questions. You will create the new you, outside the "games of the mask." Experimentation and risk-taking will challenge you to become who you want to be. And your courage will help you stay true to yourself as you learn and grow in new directions.

Human Beings' Rights

There is a movement to teach children that as human beings we each have rights, no matter what our size, age, color, sex, or religion. We all have the right to be strong, safe, and free. Most people who are grown were not taught this when they were children. Therefore, most grown people are in adult bodies but act and feel like children. It is no wonder it is difficult to pass on concepts about basic human rights to our children. Being rid of the external and internal bully/victim patterns helps us to begin to learn for ourselves how to really be strong, safe, and free. Whether or not we have children, what a legacy it will be to leave for the next generations the *example* of how to live outside of the bully/victim pattern. Future human beings have choices. They can spend their energy on healing the planet and being filled with joy, instead of having to spend so much of their lives healing themselves, the way we are having to do.

Being an Adult

An underlying theme that people who play either bully or victim roles have in common is that neither type is willing to take responsibility for their issues. In this way, people wearing the bully/victim masks are able to continue to play childlike games rather than act like grown ups.

To be truly outside the game of bully/victim requires that we act like *real* adults. Real adults are not bullies or victims. They do not need to hide behind those masks. **Being adult means taking full responsibility for our beliefs, feelings, and actions now—no matter what our past has been.**

It can be useful to examine our childhood and other past events to see what got us to this point. We can get insight into who we are. We can see if there are patterns which create constant themes in our lives. And we can recover feelings which we may have suppressed.

But the fact is that looking at the past only helps us to see our patterns and what lessons are there for us which we are still repeating *now*. Whatever happened to us 30 years ago, 5 years ago, or even 1 year ago, does not need to have a bearing on our choices in this moment. If we get stuck in playing the past tapes over and over, we deny our present responsibility to end old patterns.

At some point, we must say to ourselves, "Okay, enough raking the past over the coals. What am I going to do to take charge of the situation so I can get on with my life? I am no longer a child. I control my own destiny now." Affirming this can be the turning point toward just letting go of the whys and unsticking us from current internal bullying and victimization behavior.

This is not to say that being an adult means that we can no longer act or feel like children. The great part of being an adult is that we can *choose* to be anyone we want. But instead of being the helpless scared child from our past, we can now allow our playful, carefree child to live with us in the present. We can live in the here and now free from past fear. Choosing to be unstuck from our past allows us to have the full range of adult possibilities and say goodbye to the bully and victim.

What Real Adults Are Like

It is easy to say that we must be adults and take responsibility for our issues. But being and acting like real adults will take awareness and practice to actually accomplish. Here are some of the qualities of real adults:

Adults listen to their inner wisdom.

Adults trust themselves, so they are willing to listen to their inner truth. They know that their truth has innate wisdom. They are willing to follow it no matter what outside sources tell them to do differently.

Adults do not blame.

Adults do not blame others because they take responsibility for their own thoughts, feelings, and actions. They know that blame is like a ball and chain around their leg. Without blame, adults are free to use their energy to learn lessons from life's situations and move on. They are able to see others stuck in blame and view it as the ridiculous, childish game that it really is.

Adults do not find fault.

Adults know that finding fault with others is not only a waste of time, but it also keeps them from having the real connections with others that they want. Without fault-finding, adults have a lot more compassion for others. Instead of seeing faults, they see wounds. Why would they want to pick at someone's wounds? Real adults want to nurture wounds, not aggravate them.

Adults realize the difference between judgment and discrimination.
Adults do not judge others' thoughts, feelings, or actions. They know that they do not know the entire story, or what the future holds, so they are not in a position to understand all that is going on. Adults use their inner wisdom to discriminate between which people and circumstances are beneficial or harmful to them. Adults know that judging is based on external information, while discrimination is based on internal information.

Adults know when to draw on internal resources and when to reach out for help or comfort.
Because adults trust themselves, they are able to determine when they need to do things on their own and when they need to reach out for a comforting, helping hand from others.

There is no need for the stubborn pride of "I can do it all alone." because adults know that no person is an island. Part of what makes our human existence so magnificent is our connections to others. Adults recognize that to ask for help is sometimes the real sign of courage and strength. Adults are willing to show their imperfections, so that they can better themselves.

But adults also know when they can no longer lean on others. They have to go it alone, so they can show themselves that they do have the answers, the ability, and the creativity to take care of themselves as real adults. Adults see that there is a balance of giving to oneself and getting from others. This makes them know that the world is a safe and loving place to be, no matter where they turn for help.

Adults are not attached to outcomes.
Adults realize that it is the process of life which is important, not the outcomes. Goals are important to set. But much of why we set them is to get experiences along the way. If goals are reached, they are a nice bonus.

This principle applies in work, relationships, and everything else that is done. In relationships, it is especially evident that there is no end goal. Once a goal is reached, new goals seem to appear. So life simply becomes an unfolding story with us writing the chapters as we go.

Adults know this, so they do not get disappointed if the goal changes or is not reached. They know that whatever happens will be perfect just the way it is, even when the short-term story does not turn out the way they hoped it would.

Adults give up the need to be right.
Adults do not need to prove themselves "right." They know that there is no single right way. There are as many right ways as there are people. Adults realize that like the three blind men feeling different

parts of the elephant, each of us can be "right" from our own perspective. Since adults do not need to be "right" there is no need to defend their position. The time which some would spend in endless debate can instead be spent doing what they want to fulfill their lives.

Adults are open to new ways of perceiving the world.
Without the need to be "right" adults are open to other ways to perceive the world. They are not trapped in narrow outdated views or monotonous routines. Every experience is a new experience, making life more interesting and fun.

Adults allow others to make their own decisions about life.
Adults live their own lives to the fullest, so they have no need to live other people's lives for them. This means that they do not take responsibility for others and they do not give others advice unless asked.

Adults know that others sometimes need to make their own mistakes, to get the full impact of their lessons. While adults are there to give a helping hand, they do not interfere or try to control others. It is only an illusion which makes people believe that they can control others. Adults know this. They respect people who do exactly what needs to be done, even when appearances may show otherwise.

Adults are good listeners.

Adults are good listeners. They do not need to try to impress others with what they know and they do not need to be the center of attention.

Adults know that more is gained from listening than talking. Listening creates a receptive mode which opens us to new information and experiences with people.

Listening lets others know they are cared for. When others feel heard, they are more likely to be open and receptive to learning new ways. Adults know that they nurture others more just by being there, than by giving them all the lectures and advice in the world.

Adults are pleased to see others succeed.

Adults are happy with themselves, so they are happy to see others succeed. They do not feel jealousy, envy, or anger toward others. If they "lose" to others, they take it in stride. They appreciate the learning experience which they have gotten from the situation and feel no malice toward people who best them.

Adults celebrate others' success. They know that others' success is a sign that they, too, can achieve the same success if chosen. Adults appreciate others leading the way for them. And they are willing to express their thanks openly to others.

Adults love unconditionally.

Adults are as unconditionally loving of other people as they are of their own children. Adults are able to separate out the behavior from the people underneath. They see temper tantrums, screaming, jealousy, and revenge as behavior indicating emotional pain. Adult do not condemn people who show their pain. If the behavior impacts others, adults will show that the form of expressing the emotion may not be acceptable. But they validate that the people are entitled to whatever emotion is felt.

Becoming an Adult

Becoming an adult is a process, not necessarily an end goal. It may take some of us an entire lifetime to be adult. There are some things we can do which may help speed along our process if we are willing to do them. Mentioned here are some ideas which you may want to consider:

Find models for adult behavior
There are real adults in the world. Look around and find the people who act like adults. This does not mean that you should idealize others. It means that you observe the *parts* of their behavior which you believe fit your understanding of an adult. Try that behavior on yourself, to see if it fits. If you like it keep it, if you don't, throw it out and keep looking.

Remember, no one else has their whole act together, so if you find yourself wanting to emulate someone else's total behavior, chances are you are putting him/her on a pedestal and are not seeing the real person.

Reprogram internal negative talk

For many of us there is a constant internal chatter which consists mainly of negative things we say about ourselves. We discussed in an earlier chapter the kinds of things we say to ourselves which can be very destructive, even if said occasionally.

The negative talk can be reprogrammed over time by replacing it with new, more positive thoughts.

Put the past in the past

As long as we are stuck in the past, we are trapped in the "mask's lying contract" from which we want to escape. To be truly an adult requires that we quit mucking around in what is over and done. We have to let whatever happened go, so we can live in the present. We must get to the point of being able to say, "Okay, I get the lesson. I see what I could have done differently. Now it's time to move on." In other words, we must forgive ourselves and others for the past.

Forgiveness of ourselves and others may take time and might not feel possible for us in the early stages of shedding our mask. But to be free and to take charge of our lives, we must forgive at some point.

Forgiveness does not mean excusing behavior. It only means dropping the need to cling to the past. Freedom from the past means letting go of the anger and guilt we felt for playing the games which were manufactured to trap us in the bully and victim roles.

Nurture the inner wounded child

Because we may not have been parented in the way that best nurtured our inner child, we may still carry childhood wounds with us as grown ups. Learning how to parent ourselves is one of the main tasks of the person striving to be a real adult. Only when the child feels safe and cared for, will it let go of the mask that has been its source of protection.

There is a lot of current literature about nurturing your internal wounded child. You may want to consult those books which will help you learn, in a more detailed way, how to do that.

Talking with the parts of ourselves

Much of the internal talk with ourselves is like talking to a whole room full of people. We have an inner child and adult. But we may also have an internal tyrant, critic, wimp, complainer, nag, artist, genius, idiot, etc. Sometimes there is a cacophony of competition for air space between all of our inner voices.

Under all of those louder voices is our internal sage who does not compete for space. It simply waits for the silence. It waits to be asked its wise perspective which has been there all along.

Helping ourselves to quiet the voices sometimes may feel like parents dealing with their children. One of the obvious things to do with children who constantly talk, is to give them full attention. Sometimes that is the only thing they want. Once you are focusing attention their direction, they stop talking.

As we begin to deal with our inner voices, we may find that we have "raised" very unruly voices. They are totally without discipline and they are acting like internal bullies. If we deal with these internal bullies as if they are undisciplined children, we may begin to see a change over time in their disruptive behavior. Some examples of things you may want to say to your bullying voices are:

1. "This behavior is unacceptable. If you can't behave, you'll have to leave the room."
2. "You are obviously in a bad mood. It's not okay for you to drag down the rest of us. You'll have to go off by yourself, if you want to be negative."
3. "We want to have a good time and enjoy ourselves right now. We'll listen to you later, but for now we will not sacrifice our good time to deal with the negativity."
4. "*You* are very loved, but this *specific behavior* is unacceptable."
5. "Do you know why you are choosing to feel this way?"
6. "What will you do, to decide to feel better?"

We may also find parts of ourselves that have been so damaged that they barely have voices at all, because of their pain. They are not bullies and they will need to be treated gently, like lifting newborn babies from earthquake ruins. We will need to cuddle them, and coo over them. We will want to rock them, stroke them, and sing to them. Imagine taking these parts of ourselves in our arms and saying, "I'm so sorry I wasn't able to be there for you sooner. But I am here now, and I will protect you. You are safe." This will go a long way to helping the scared parts of ourselves feel safe again.

Just as parents cannot treat all children in the family alike because of differences in personality, we cannot treat all of our internal parts alike. It is our task as adults to figure out how to treat each part, so that all parts get the best nurturing possible.

Practice dialogues with others in a safe environment

Learning how to be an adult when dealing with others outside of ourselves will take practice. Obviously, there will be trial and error.

Sometimes there is a need to practice in a safe environment before trying the real thing on actual people in our lives. This way we can check to see how we feel and decide what we need to do differently to feel like we are being adults. We may want to practice these dialogues with a friend, our spouse, a family member, or a therapist. Whoever is selected should love us and be someone we trust not to hurt us or manipulate us when we expose our wounds.

GOODBYE BULLY, GOODBYE VICTIM

While there is responsibility which comes with being an adult, there is immense freedom as well. Ties to the games of bully/victim disappear. We no longer allow the mask to dictate our lives, because as adults we choose to be whoever we want to be.

CHAPTER 10
Turning Gullibility into Wisdom

*"If you don't stand for something,
you'll fall for anything."*
Author Unknown

We have examined some of the ways manipulators are able to read gullible people so easily. Just the awareness of what manipulators see in us helps us to end our own gullibility. But there are techniques which we can use to go to new levels of dealing with the world around us.

"Red Flags" Signaling Manipulation

Within us we have "red flags" which act as our early warning detection devices to alert us to potential manipulation. Paying attention to the "red flags" will allow us time to deal with situations in other ways, so we don't get sucked into the mask's game of manipulation.

Red flag 1:
   If we *feel* like saying or doing one thing, but *actually* say or do something else instead.
   Any time we have felt something and reacted the opposite of our feelings, we have set ourselves up for manipulation. Here are some examples of how we sabotage ourselves:

a. **We override our intuition with old "should" or "ought to" tapes.**
Example: Mary is asked by her husband, Alvin, what she wants for their anniversary. What comes to Mary's mind is "a divorce." What she says to Alvin is, "a cookbook."

b. **We don't want to be perceived as weak, so we do what we believe will be perceived by others as strong.**
Example: Henry feels overwhelmed with so many projects at work. He is trying to figure out how he is going to get all of his work done when his boss, Frank, comes into his office. Frank says, "Henry, I always know I can count on you to pull us out of the fire. I have a special project I want to assign to you which is due next week. For the sake of the team, can you show us what you're made of on this one?" Henry wants to scream and say, "No way can I take on another project. You have got to be crazy!" What Henry actually says is, "Sure, you can always count on me."

c. **We want to avoid conflict.**
Example: Raymond is engrossed in a football game on T.V. when his wife, Margaret, says,"I'm going to the mall for some shopping. I really want you to go with me, so we can spend some time together." Raymond hates malls and shopping. He doesn't want to leave the game he is watching. Besides, when Margaret is shopping she never pays attention

to him, so they are not really together. But when Raymond looks at Margaret with disgust, Margaret screams, "You never want to be with me." Silently, she says, "I'll make your life a living hell if you don't go with me. You know that, don't you?" Raymond remembers the last time they had this argument. Margaret snapped at him for a week afterward. Raymond turns to Margaret and says, "Why, of course I'd love to go to the mall with you, dear."

When we stop overriding our natural responses, we will put a significant dent in others' ability to manipulate us. Even if it is difficult to stay true to our feelings in the beginning, the more we practice, the easier it gets. Eventually we will be able to let others' attempts at manipulation roll off us completely.

Red flag 2:
If we feel anxious, claustrophobic, itchy, trapped, creepy, or restless. Our body may be warning us that we need to get away from a person or situation.

Example: Kathleen is out on a blind date with Bill, a neighbor's friend. Bill invites Kathleen to his house for a drink. Kathleen feels like saying no, but is afraid Bill will be offended, so she agrees to go to his house. She doesn't know why, but feels very restless and claustrophobic while at Bill's place. The

166

whole time there, Kathleen feels like making a dash for the front door. She also finds herself looking at the windows. But she does not follow what her body tells her, which is to leave. She stays. Bill "date rapes" Kathleen that night. Too late, she knows why she felt uncomfortable and wanted to leave.

When we are in the middle of a situation and get a body warning, we may not know why we feel it. But if we pay attention to our warning signs, without waiting for an answer to why we feel that way, we can avoid a potential danger. We will probably never know if something really would have happened. But the mystery is better than later finding out, like Kathleen did, that her instincts were right.

Red flag 3:

If we feel numb, immobilized, tongue-tied, or confused. Our mind could be saying, we need to take a break to figure out what is going on. Some of the things our mind may be trying to figure out are:

a. We are scared and need to find a safe way to deal with the person or situation.

Example: Christine's partner, Kurt, screams whenever they have a fight. Kurt screams at Christine inches from her face. Christine becomes very numb and frightened. She feels like a stone statue and is unable to think, speak, or even move. The only choice Christine feels that she has, when Kurt screams, is to brace herself for his "hurricane of emotions" to blow over. She usually breaks down into tears after his screaming and runs into the bedroom to hide from him. Christine needs more physical space between herself and Kurt when they fight. Extra space would make her feel safe enough to speak her mind without feeling like his fury will be dumped on her. Christine's numbness keeps her from directly facing her fright issues.

b. **We feel rushed into a decision and need time to think about it away from others.** **Example**: Jerry gets very frustrated with himself whenever he is around Wilma, his boss. Jerry is a very slow and methodical worker who is very detail-oriented and precise. Wilma is the type of person who is always in a hurry and operates on tight schedules and deadlines. Wilma doesn't think of details. That's what she hired Jerry to do. Jerry very often feels tongue-tied and muddled when he talks to Wilma. He is afraid Wilma thinks he is stupid because of his behavior. Jerry is unaware that he feels rushed by Wilma and doesn't want to make snap decisions about major projects. This could effect the smooth running of the department and the product sold to customers. He needs time to think through the details to determine whether Wilma's ideas will actually work.

c. **We need to sort out our feelings and get to our own truth of the situation.**
Example: Sonia has been dissatisfied with her job as a retail store manager for some time, but is not sure why. Her husband, David, calls her at work excited to tell her that he has been offered a very good-paying job in a small town, in another part of the state. He thinks that Sonia will be anxious to go because she doesn't like her job anyway. Instead Sonia says, "I don't know why, but I don't want to go. I'm confused. I can't think." David is baffled. So is Sonia. She doesn't feel like she has logical reasons why she's not willing to move. What Sonia hasn't been willing to acknowledge to herself yet, is that she really wants to go to law school. The only school nearby is in the town where they currently reside. If they move to the small town across the state, she won't be able to go to law school.

If we give ourselves time to figure out what we are feeling, we will often be able to express it to the people we deal with in a much more precise way. The extra time allows the answer to come from our truth. It may help us to remember that no one else can make us adhere to *their* timetables or decision-making process. We own and display our feelings, not theirs. It is up to us to decide how we want to be.

Red flag 4:
If we express one emotion, but really feel another emotion.
Because of our own past history, or what we believe is "acceptable" behavior, we may feel that it is okay to express only certain emotions. There may be one emotion which we totally suppress. Often it is the one we are really feeling and is the one which most needs to be expressed.
a. We want to get angry but instead we cry.
Example: Denise has been called into her boss's office to be given her evaluation. She feels that she has done a very good job during the evaluation period. Her boss, Julie, hands her the evaluation. She has been given "needs improvement" consistently on all sections. Denise is furious. She knows that the low marks have nothing to do with her job performance, but the fact that she and Julie had a falling out on a personal matter several months ago and are no longer close friends like they once were. Denise finds that in spite of her effort to hold back tears, they start rolling down her face. She is embarrassed to be crying in an evaluation, but can't help it. What Denise is not paying attention to is that she is so angry that she is afraid if she opens her mouth, venomous rage will pour out. She has been trained from the time she was a little

girl that "nice" girls don't get angry. Denise feels that the only outlet for her rage is through her tear ducts.

b. **We want to feel sad but instead we get angry.**
Example: Jordon has just gotten a phone call from his brother that his father died. For an instant, Jordon feels like crying, but he pushes back the feeling almost as soon as it starts to flood into him. A stern voice within him reminds him, "Big boys don't cry." Jordon finds himself raising his voice to his brother, "How dare Dad die right now and leave Mom all alone. He always was a selfish old coot. And of course, you know who will be stuck taking care of Mom. It'll be me since I live so close. I can't believe he just up and died on us!" Even though he is 45 years old, Jordon feels like a child abandoned by his father, but won't let himself feel the sadness over the loss. He covers it with what he learned was an "appropriate male emotion," anger.

Awareness that we are feeling one emotion and expressing another is a very important step in ending our manipulation. By learning to express our whole range of natural emotions, we can allow ourselves a fuller spectrum of responses to situations. Having more choices helps us to feel more in charge of our lives and no longer at the mercy of others.

Red flag 5:
If we operate on automatic pilot without awareness of what we are feeling, thinking, or doing. Operating as if we are in a dreamlike state or a haze will mean that we are more likely to be manipulated by others who are aware of our "unawareness."
Example: Jack has just gotten home from work and has turned on the television and opened the newspaper. He has disengaged his brain from work, but not yet tuned in to what is happening with the family. He is sitting in a semi-comatose state when his teenage daughter, Debra, asks if she can go on a date tonight and use the car. Jack says yes without thinking about the fact that Debra is grounded for a week. He is also oblivious that it is a school night and Debra is not permitted to go out on school nights. Of course, Debra knew her father would be "out of it" at this time of night. That's why she asked him when she did.
By becoming aware of times when we know we cannot realistically make decisions or engage our brains, we can tell others that we are not open for discussing things at that time. Simply putting this in the back of our mind can allow our awareness to engage enough to not be manipulated.

Red flag 6:
If we feel smaller than the other peı son or not a peer with *any* *other* adult. As adults we are every other adult's peer. Only by believing or acting differently can we hide this truth from ourselves. There is a lot of emphasis in our society on putting one another in a pecking order according to social status, job or title held, educational level, race, sex, etc.

Example: Bob is the boss in a department of his company. He loves being very dictatorial with his staff because he doesn't want them to forget that he is their boss. He periodically walks around his department to "inspect the troops," so he can keep them in line. Bob is walking through his department one day with his chest puffed out when Tony, his boss, walks in. Immediately, Bob's demeanor changes. He stoops his shoulders and lowers his eyes. He falls in line behind Tony like a puppy behind its owner. Bob says, "Yes, sir" frequently and reflects back whatever Tony says to him. Although Bob sees himself on the top of the pecking order with his staff, he feels he is on the bottom of the heap with the supervisors above him. He does not see himself as a peer to anyone else in the company.

We are all equal in our status as adult human beings. Whenever we find ourselves feeling inferior to someone, we are likely to also be showing gullibility to their control on some level. If we feel superior, then chances are we will be more likely to manipulate others either on purpose or inadvertently. If we pay attention to how we feel about ourselves around others, we will begin to see if we really believe we are a peer with others. If we feel like a peer, that will be radiated to everyone around us and we will be more likely to be treated as one human being to another.

What is Needed to Turn Gullibility into Wisdom

To turn our gullibility into wisdom requires a good hard look at ourselves and others. We must see everyone as real people and not the illusions we have created. This will mean examining our needs, desires, insecurities, senses of lack, negative inner voices, and anything else rolled into the package called us.

There is a sorting out process which happens as we start to unwrap our package. As we examine all aspects of ourselves, we can see what are really our truths, what are others which we have taken on as ours, and what are questionable. It may be like sorting the laundry with three baskets labelled, "keep 'em," "trash 'em," and "question 'em." The unwrapping process is the one which is the most difficult for many of us. We may be afraid of things in our package which we don't like. But developing confidence and personal skills can help us face ourselves as we shed our gullibility.

Personal Skills for Living Beyond Gullibility

Rising above our gullibility means that we no longer need to feel like a victim mashed under the heel of an oppressive giant. It means when we see manipulative behavior, we give a clear message without any words, "I see what you are trying to do, but it won't work with me." We trade in our neon gullibility sign for one which says, "Manipulators not welcome. Go away." Here are some of the skills you can use to rid yourself of gullibility. If practiced, you will begin to see your wisdom blossom as your gullibility withers away.

Be the observer of your own situations

It is often easy to see when other people are suckered. But we fail to see our own gullibility, because we are so immersed in the situation that we don't see the larger perspective. Developing the observer portion of ourselves can keep us from getting sucked into the manipulators' grip. The observer is that "higher" portion of ourselves which can see what we do objectively. We can picture our observer sitting in the corner of the room, or somewhere above us. We ask our observer to notify us if we start to do anything that smacks of gullibility. Some people have the observer shake their shoulder, whisper in their ear, or shout, if necessary, to get our attention. The job of the observer is to draw our attention out of the details of the event, and see what we are about to do.

From the observer vantage point, here are some of the things you may be able to use to help you discontinue your gullibility:

1. **See where you get "hooked" by the manipulator.**
   a. Listen to the manipulator from the perspective of the feelings inside you. If you have a tug in your gut or a flash of an image while the manipulator is saying something to you, note this for later examination.
   b. Be alert for any "red flags" which you may be trying to give yourself, as signs that you are needing to pay attention to.
   c. Examples of how manipulators hook us are: our desire to be loyal, our need to be perceived as intelligent, our fear for personal safety, our need to be nice, patriotic, good caretakers, etc. Objectively examine where manipulators hook you without judging yourself.

2. **See manipulators for who they really are.**
   a. See manipulators as caricatures of their real selves.
   Remember some of the common masks we examined in Chapter 3. See if any of these fit. Or better yet, come up with your own

caricatures which fit the manipulators in your life. You may not take their manipulations as seriously, or even believe them, if you do this.
b. See the manipulators' wounded inner child. You may not like the behavior of manipulators. But if you see the manipulations as attempts to cover their inner wounded child, your gullibility will begin to be replaced by compassion. **When you have compassion, all of the energy is taken out of the manipulation and it has no power.** You may not find the manipulative behavior acceptable, but you are still able to love the person underneath who feels so desperate that he or she needs to manipulate.

Stay centered

As we discussed earlier, we are innately balanced at the level of our essence. But when we are feeling gullible, it is difficult for us to get in touch with our internal gyroscope. Here are some of the things you can do in dealing with others to strip away the weight which throws your gyroscope off balance:

1. Become a responder instead of a reactor.

When we *react* we are reading what is going on in the world outside of us and acting based on external factors. When we *respond* we are reading what is going on inside of us, and acting based on our internal truth and reality. Or stated more simply:

Reaction comes from *outside* of us.

Response comes from *inside* of us.

To some who aren't familiar with this concept, it may sound like only semantics. But for those who understand and live by the response principle, there is an internal peace which begins to be present no matter what the situation. The following may help to illustrate the distinction.

Example: Tim is a pitcher in the last inning of a baseball championship game. The bases are loaded with two strikes. As he winds up for what may be the final pitch of the game, the opposing team's fans start calling him names and jeer him. They yell, "Choke. Choke. Choke."

Tim reacts. He loses his concentration by looking up in the stands to see who called him names. He gets angry. He throws the pitch but it is wild. He is still distracted by the fans. He does indeed choke in the clutch.

Tim responds. He blocks out all outside distractions. He is completely focused. He is one with the ball visualizing it going over home plate and the umpire calling "Strike three." Tim throws the pitch and knows before the ball reaches the plate that his team has won the game.

The difference between reaction and response is not reserved only for the athlete or a special circumstance. It can be profound in day-to-day dealings in everything you do. It may take practice to be a responder, but the change will be noticeable to everyone around you. Being a responder means that no one, and nothing can rock you off your foundation.

2. **Let others hurt, anger, bad mood, and negative energy roll off of you.** Most people have been trained to be like emotional velcro strips. When others throw their barbed emotions our direction, we let them stick to us. When we are centered, we pluck off all of the negative feelings others have tossed to us. We eventually take off our velcro strips entirely so no energy is invested defending ourselves against other's negativity. To do this, we must first become aware of how, when, and where in our body we take in the negativity. Then we can begin to practice techniques for keeping the negativity from sticking. Other images may be more helpful for you in this process such as:

1. Picture that you are teflon and everything negative that others say or do slides off. Only the positive is let in.
2. Imagine others' negativity being like blow darts. When the darts approach you, you catch them in midair and throw them to the ground.
3. See yourself with a catcher's mitt. Grab any negativity coming your direction and send it back where it came from.

4. See others throwing negativity your way but miss you. It is deflected because of a powerful force field you create surrounding you. Once you get used to stopping others' negativity from wounding you at a deep level, you may find that much of it will go away. Some people won't send it to you anymore, because they can't get you to play their game. They will either quit playing the game, or find new players.

Other people will continue to send negativity your direction. But, if you don't take it, no matter how much they try, their negativity won't affect you. When you are unhooked from them, then you can make clear choices about whether you really want consistently negative people in your life.

3. **Set clear boundaries so you can feel safe, strong and free.**

We discussed in the last chapter about having the "human right" to feel safe, strong, and free. To exercise these rights we must set clear boundaries for ourselves, so that we will not feel invaded by others. This is a real key to turning our gullibility into wisdom. When we are gullible, we let manipulators know that the door to our home is wide open and they can take whatever they like. It is no wonder that we feel so violated when we allow ourselves to be manipulated.

180

TURNING GULLIBILITY INTO WISDOM

Setting clear boundaries for ourselves is crucial for us to end the feeling of being violated. It may take time to internally get clear about where our boundaries are. Noticing where we feel safe is a start for establishing boundaries. Questions we may want to ask ourselves to clarify our natural boundaries are:
   a. When I am talking to a stranger, how physically close can they be for me to still feel comfortable?
   b. How physically (mentally, emotionally) close can I be to someone who knows me very well?
   c. When someone is angry with me, how close to them can I be and still feel safe?
   d. How comfortable am I when I am touched by a stranger, friend, lover, etc.?
   e. When I am with others, do I feel a clear sense of myself as a separate person?

By asking these questions and any others that come to mind, you will begin to become aware of your safety zones which keep you from feeling violated. If this seems to be an important issue for you, you may want to read books on the market about boundaries or find a therapist who can help you develop a clear sense of your personal boundaries.

Develop common sense
   A typical reason for gullibility is because common sense is overridden. To more fully rely on your

common sense requires that you combine your intelligence and intuition so that you learn to be discriminating. This does not mean rigidly seeing all people in a particular way. It does mean using your intelligence and intuition to determine if a *particular* situation is one which is helpful for you or not. If you trust all bankers because your father was a banker and you believe they must be honest to be in banking, you are not using your common sense. You also will be setting yourself up to fall prey to a manipulator. Instead, if you talk to a particular banker and feel after questioning that he or she *individually* is trustworthy, you are more likely using your common sense.

Don't accept the manipulation contract

For there to be a manipulation contract, the gullible person has to accept it. If it is not accepted, there is no contract. Simple as that.

The only power that manipulators have is the power they get from those who are willing to be gullible. So if you keep your power and refuse to give it to manipulators, they are impotent. They are then left to deal with their own impotence, and will have to face their own consequences for not taking responsibility for their lives.

When you hand them back their own manipulative energy, you have called "emperor's new clothes" on them. You will have shown courage where others have not. You also are letting them know that they are capable of handling their own needs and desires without giving the responsibility away. You are saying they are peers. That is one of the best gifts you can give to any other adult.

Facing the manipulator

We will get many lessons facing would-be manipulators in our lives. Seeing these challenges as learning opportunities can help us encounter them without feeling that our gullibility is too threatening. Here are some reminders when dealing with manipulators:

1. Sort out whose issues are whose. If it is their problem, let them face their own consequences.
2. Know that it is all right to say no, or tell others to stop.
3. It is okay to walk away if you feel you need to. Do not judge yourself as a coward. Sometimes leaving is the *prudent* thing to do.
4. Pay attention to your gut reactions. Remember the "red flags" your intuition may be telling you.
5. Don't allow others to rush you into decisions.
6. Know it is okay for you to change your mind, no matter how much others try to pressure you.
7. *Others' reality is not your reality.* Their reality may not make any sense to you because it doesn't belong to you. That's okay. It doesn't have to make sense to anyone else but them. If you let others convince you that their reality is the "correct" one, you may feel like there is something wrong with your reality. Trying to understand their reality, in too much detail, can

divert your energy away from your own life. (It won't really help them figure out how to live their lives, because they must do that for themselves.)

8. Deal with a situation and then let it go. Beating yourself about the past only damages you and does not help you learn the lesson.

9. Use humor to lighten up the situation. Sometimes letting others know in a playful way that you see what they are trying to do and are not taking them seriously can diffuse the situation and end it very quickly.

Learn to trust yourself more than anyone else

To be truly free of gullibility, you have to trust yourself more than you trust any other human being on the face of the earth. This means trusting yourself even more than others who love you immensely, like your parents, spouse, or best friends. You must be willing to rely on your own perceptions, judgment, and knowledge of yourself and the world.

Trusting yourself does not mean that you have to mistrust others, though. When you decide that you really want to trust yourself, you may not yet feel totally trustworthy. Getting support from others to help you develop self-trust, may be what is called for.

During the time of building self-trust, there may be situations which challenge the self-trust you feel that you already have. That is part of the natural process of expanding your truth. You may find that others sometimes say things which tap a raw nerve within you. This may be a sign that there is still a part of you which you do not yet trust completely. You can use others' challenges as opportunities to do more in-depth examination so you can learn to completely trust yourself.

Communication Beyond Gullibility or Manipulation

Understanding the masks that others wear can help us separate the behavior from the actual people. When we are able to do this we can then challenge their behavior, but nurture their truth. This requires us to:

Listen to the real messages

We can ask ourselves what others are *really* wanting from us? They may not be aware of what that is. But if we allow ourselves to know what they want, we may understand them better than they understand themselves. When we can do this, our gullibility is nonexistent.

Let others know we understand their manipulative game and don't choose to play

Sometimes we may need to say very clearly, "No, I don't choose to be manipulated today, thank you." Other times we can more subtly let others know that we understand what they are doing and we do not want to play their game. This requires us to be clear and firm within ourselves. We must stay in our own clear energy and not let ourselves be diverted by manipulation. This may take practice. But the clearer we get, the less forcefully we will have to communicate our message verbally. Our presence will let others know that we can no longer be batted around by their game.

Drop judgement and replace it with insight
When we first begin to see the manipulation of others for what it is, we may feel very betrayed. How could people we trusted and loved take advantage of our weaknesses and use them against us? Why would they do that to *us*? We may be very angry and judge them as being bad or mean people. These feelings are natural and may be signs that we have taken the first step to ending our gullibility.

But at some point, to get rid of our gullibility and learn to communicate with others from a place of strength, we will need to go beyond judging manipulative people as bad people. We will need to see them as hurt people who haven't figured out how to give to themselves what they really want. Allowing our energy to release judgement, frees us to understand others. Knowing the real people under the manipulation (even if we do not agree with or like the manipulation itself) is an important step in true communication. When people feel truly understood, they feel validated. Validated people are less defensive or offensive. They don't need to manipulate to get what they want.

Keep an open heart and clear boundaries

What many people do when they figure out they have been gullible is to shut down their hearts to others. They may hold onto the anger and feelings of betrayal which only makes them eventually become bitter, crusty people who are unable to connect with others.

To keep this from happening to us requires that we maintain an open heart to love others and keep clear boundaries for ourselves. There is a real act of love for ourselves and manipulative people when we communicate nonverbally, "I love your essence *and* I will not allow your manipulative behavior to wound me." At some level they want to end the charade and be real. Having love for them and clear boundaries helps this to happen.

Claiming Our Wisdom

Wisdom is the power of judging rightly and following the prudent course of action, based on knowledge, experience, and understanding. Wisdom implies becoming an astute observer of human nature. The wise person clearly sees situations and people as they truly are, not as they present themselves. To view others with this clarity means that we can trust again. Then we are trusting *our own knowledge,* rather than what others tell us.

Wisdom requires reclaiming our straight-line connection to our own truth. And it also requires *reconnecting our intuition and reasoning.* Once we have our connection firmly reestablished, no one will be able to manipulate us by offering to step in and make that connection for us.

CHAPTER 11
Trading Fear for Freedom

*"Fear is really a call for help,
and therefore a request for love."*
Gerald Jampolsky

Why Release Fear

Fear is what keeps us playing the "games of the mask." Fear and intimidation are the only tools that the mask has to bind us. Once we release fear, we are free. Free to love ourselves and others. Free to pursue our dreams. Free to experience life in a boundless way.

We need to release fear to free our essence from bondage. Once fear is gone, our essence cannot be held back by the mask and will simply see the ways of the mask as a bad dream.

Releasing fear allows us to feel like adults, on an equal ground with every other adult. No longer will we need to bully or be cowed by others' behavior. We will not need to present a facade of being stronger or weaker than we really are. We will be proud of ourselves, wounds and all.

Releasing fear means that we can feel good again. Our body will no longer be stuck in fear. It can relax. It can instead begin soaking up experiences, feeling the poetry of life.

When we rid ourselves of fear, we rid ourselves of anxiety, agitation, dread, apprehension, and terror of life. Our perception will no longer be distorted or confused about reality. We will no longer have to torture ourselves trying to fit into other people's view of the world around us.

Fear keeps us trapped in the past or afraid of the future. Both past and future deny us of the present, which is the only reality that we really have. Both past and future are illusions. Only the present moment has any meaning.

And releasing the fear frees up our energy, to begin to feel the love and joy around us. Once we are more relaxed without fear, we start to find the lighter side of life and have fun again.

In his book, *Love is Letting Go of Fear*, Gerald Jampolsky said it very well, "With love as our only reality, health and wholeness can be viewed as inner peace, and healing can be seen as letting go of fear."*

Why Do We Have Fear?

Fear is an attempt to warn us that we are unsafe. Sometimes it is well founded, but many times it is not. What we have to do is get to the root of the fear. Then we can determine if the thing we are scared of is really something which we need to be afraid of, or if we can change our perception and release the fear.

Do you remember when you were a child ever seeing shadows in the dark and imagining a monster or the boogy man present? All you had to do was

---

* Gerald Jampolsky, *Love is Letting Go of Fear* (New York: Bantam Books, 1981), p. 18.

flip on the light to see that there was nothing there. It was in your imagination. Most adult fear is an illusion just like when we were children. It feels real to us because we are very good at creating realistic illusions. We are also influenced by others who are having the same illusions. But once we flip on the light of awareness, we see that there really is nothing to be frightened of.

Part of the task of releasing the fear is to separate out the realistic fears from the illusory ones. This requires willingness to look deeply within ourselves. Then we can decide if we want to continue living inside a haunted house, or to walk freely in the world.

Realistic Versus Illusionary Fears

Realistic Fears	Illusionary Fears
•"If I step in front of a moving bus, I might die."	•"If I lose this job, I'll be a homeless person."
•"If I drink and drive, I might cause an accident or hurt someone."	•"I'm so fat, I'll never get anyone to marry me."
•"If I take drugs during my pregnancy, I might risk the health of the baby."	•"I can't go out at night because I will be killed."

Where Fear Comes From

Our fear in the present comes from many different sources. One of our best sources of fear is our own past experiences which we labelled as "bad." Any time we start to do something which reminds us of the past, we simply pull out the "bad" experience and say to ourselves, "Oh, no. I'm not going to experience that again."

We may have gotten fears from our parents or other family members when we were growing up. If we saw our parents be fearful of certain things, we may also have those same fears. If, for instance, our mother was bitten by a dog when she was young, she may never have gotten over her fear of dogs. She may have taught us that we "should" be frightened of dogs. Any time we got a "should" or "ought to," it probably was a message grounded in fear.

As adults, we no longer need to have our parents around to tell us the things we "should" be afraid of. We have incorporated their messages into our own internal tape bank and now can play back all the "shoulds" and "ought to's" whenever we are up for a good scare.

Society is also a great source to draw on for messages about fear. People we encounter at work, church, community groups, neighbors, and even people at the bus stop will gladly add to our tape bank of fear, if we allow them. We see fear exhibited in T.V. sit coms, in novels, and at the movies. Fear can be given to us in great abundance by those around us. Like nuclear stockpiles, most people have more fear than they could possibly ever need.

There is a more subtle, but very important source of fear which is often overlooked. That is collective genetic memory which is held within our body. This memory has been passed to us over the generations as a human species. It is part of our instinct. An example of this source of fear would be our "fight or flight" impulse when someone attacks us.

And within families, there is also a genetic ancestral memory which is strongly imbedded in us from our specific genealogy. An example of this would be if your family has a predisposition to cancer. There may be some carried self-hatred (which is a form of fear) or other fear passed from generation to generation.

Messages Our Fear Gives Us

Our fear, as Gerald Jampolsky says, is a "call for help". It is desperately trying to tell us that there is something we are not paying attention to internally. If we listen to the surface message we hear at first, we may miss the real message beneath which is at the root of our fear. So we must really listen closely without judging the fear, to hear the small scared voice which is afraid to speak up.

Below are some examples of what our fear will tell us outwardly and the *actual* underlying messages:

Outward Reason Given for Fear	Underlying Message: Belief Behind Fear
•"I'm afraid to quit my job and start my own business."	•"I'm afraid I'll lose my partner because I've never had a good relationship and done what I like at the same time."
•"I'm scared to leave my spouse."	•"If I leave I'll be a failure and a quitter. I can't bear to fail, and I'm not a quitter."
•"I'm afraid to tell my parents I want to spend Christmas in Hawaii this year, instead of with them."	•"I am afraid my parent's disapproval will mean I'll lose their love."

Anger as a Specific Form of Fear

There seems to be a magical quality to anger which most people tacitly agree to accept. That agreement is, "You be angry and I will be scared of you." or "You get angry, so I will get angry back."

Most people still see anger as a sign that someone is strong. In reality, most anger, especially anger disproportionate to the situation, shows that people are fearful at a very deep level. They may be fearful they won't be recognized, be heard, or get what they want. Most anger shows that people's internal and external realities are not in balance. Seeing anger as a wound which needs to be healed rather than as strength, changes our perception of how to deal with angry people and ourselves. For many people, anger toward others is a way to get really stuck and dissipate true strength. People who use anger in this way waste their energy being angry about situations and people over which they have no control. They remain angry because they are closed to receiving the real messages their anger is giving them. **The real message of anger is almost always about their own *beliefs, perceptions, or actions* in a given situation or with particular people, not the situations or people themselves.**

Conversely, when anger is denied, strength is dissipated by using available energy to keep the anger in control. When people have internal tapes which say, "It's not nice to be angry," or "I should be above anger," they deny themselves the chance to feel it fully and then release it. Without full release, denial covers over the anger keeping them from moving beyond it.

Anger toward the self can also dissipate our true strength. Almost everybody to some degree or another, is angry with themselves for not figuring out how to do some aspect of life the way they think it "should" be done. Their anger energy when directed inward acts like an ingrown hair. This is like a force pushing against our strength which is trying to get out. The resistance creates an internal struggle which also zaps our strength.

Anger exists for a reason. It *is* a powerful force. When we can direct it into constructive areas of our lives, we can recover it as a strength. It is only when it is out of control or stuck that anger harms others or ourselves.

Mind Games We Play on Ourselves to Perpetuate Fear

Over the years of living with our mask of fear, we may have developed internal mind games to perpetuate our fears. We have plenty of people in our external world who willingly teach us the mind games and urge us to continue playing them.

Mind games are simply ploys of the mask to keep us hooked into the "mask's lying contract." Once we see this we can stop the mind games which cause us to feel fearful.

Some of the common mind games we believe to perpetuate our fear:

Our perception of the world is wrong.

We begin to believe that we cannot trust what we see. Once we do this, we may suspend our belief and begin to trust others' reality more than ours. This will make us deeply fearful. This is because ripping our reality foundation out from under ourselves, makes us feel like we are on shaky ground. Also, no one else's reality ever makes sense to us because it is not ours. We may start to feel like we are walking through a mine field, ready to step on something dangerous.

They must be right–I respect them.
Just because you "respect" others does not mean that they are right. Often when people find something that works for them, they declare it as "right." But there is no "right" or "wrong" way to view the world, or to do things. There are only different individual ways.

Also sometimes our respect for others may not be well-founded. We may have set them on a pedestal. If we have done that, then we may have decided that whatever they do is the "right" thing.

We must keep in mind that everyone else is human, just like us. No one has the patent on how life *should* be lived. Otherwise, it would have been bottled and sold in K-Mart as a "blue-light special" by now. We would be well-served to get rid of all of the pedestals on which we have put anyone above us. Then we can see that others are trying to figure things out, just like we are. They certainly deserve no more (or less) respect than we give ourselves.

Everyone else is doing it, so it must be right.
Even as children when we used this excuse, we were told how foolish it was. How many times have we heard, "If they were jumping off a cliff, would you jump, too?" But it is amazing that, as adults, we

still play this mind game. We still succumb to peer pressure in the same way we did in high school. If we didn't, tyrants would not be able to control groups of people.

It is important to remember that there can be *mass delusion* because so few people are willing to take responsibility for their own perception. Just because "everybody" believes something, or acts a certain way does not mean that they are any more right as adults than it was when we were children.

Others' anger can hurt me.

The only way that others' anger will hurt us is if we let it. Since anger indicates others' frustration at not feeling good internally, there is no reason for us to feel afraid of it. But if we believe that others' anger can hurt us, it surely will.

In Vernon Howard's book, *50 Ways to See Thru People,* he states it very well:

"Listen to this! No one has power to hurt you unless you yourself supply that power by fearing him. Your own fright and unawareness is the only source of strength he has. It is like a soldier handing over his rifle to the enemy. A tyrant reacts with evil excitement at your fear, which he must have to wound you, for evil has no power of its own. So have no fear. You can actually ignore all tyrants out of existence!"**

Why do I keep beating on myself?

This is a very common mind game which keeps us in fear instead of freeing us to make the changes necessary to stop the beatings. Constant preoccupation with the "whys" only makes ourselves try harder to justify our behavior. As we discussed earlier, feeling like we need to justify ourselves is one of the ways we are exploited.

Asking too many whys means that we are being our own bully. We are telling ourselves that we will only give ourselves love if we can explain why we have been fearful. If someone goes into the emergency room with a heart attack, the nurses and doctors do not ask the patient to justify why she has had a heart attack before they will treat her. They concentrate on saving her life. At that point the whys of the heart attack are irrelevant.

The whys for us are useful to understand at some point. But concentrating our energy on the whys rather than stopping the fear, only adds to our fear that it will never end. The irony is that often when we quit beating on ourselves by asking the whys, the answers come to us without any effort.

** Vernon Howard, *50 Ways to see Thru People* (Boulder City: New Life Foundation, 1981) p. 31.

How to See Through Others to Stop Fearing Them

To start seeing through the masks of others and stop fearing them, it may be helpful to remember some of these things:

1. Others usually don't know more than you do. They are mostly bluffing.
2. Trust your instinct (intuition) over what others tell you.
3. Beware of offers for instant cures, or fixes from others.
4. Others can't give you security. It is a hoax if they pretend to.
5. You aren't responsible for others' disappointment or hurt. But they may attempt to shame you to see if you will relieve them of their issues.
6. Tyrants' and bullies' only power over you is your fear. Give up the fear and the power is gone.
7. Whatever someone is threatening you with, is probably their own deep fear. (**Example**: If our mates often threaten to leave us, they are probably afraid we will abandon them. Their threat to leave gives them a sense of control over their deep fear.)
8. Stop self-condemnation and others will never again be able to condemn or shame you.

9. Don't take what others say too seriously. (Seriousness is one of the most common "fear hooks.")
10. You are equal to everyone.

How Fear Can Affect Our Body

We discussed earlier how the body holds keys for us about our emotions and psychological makeup. Fear can specifically affect our bodies in adverse ways. Some of the ways fear is evidenced in our body are: addictions, back pain, bladder problems, headaches, indigestion, nervousness, and skin problems.*** These "problems" are a way our body is attempting to get our attention when we do not hear more subtle internal clues from our emotions or thoughts.

Many people take pain killers, and other drugs which mask the pain or may temporarily get rid of outward symptoms of fear. But without going to the underlying message our problem is giving us, we are likely to have the pain reoccur in the future. The body does not give up easily on giving us information even when we are very resistant to hearing what it has to say.

*** For more detail on how new thought patterns can lessen or eliminate physical and mental problems, see Louise Hay's book, *Heal Your Body* (Santa Monica: Hay House, 1988).

Getting Free of Fear

Releasing the Fear Gently

The process of releasing fear must be a gentle process for it to be lasting. The things that cause fear can be let go of simply by seeing them and acknowledging that we no longer need to be fearful of them. An example of this would be if we have a fear that someone is hiding under our bed. Just look under the bed. Our fear will go away when we see that there really is no one there.

Other more embedded fears may take time to release. We have to get rid of the fear at both a body and an emotional level for it to be totally gone. We may think that we have released a particular fear. But then in a later situation, we have the same fear present itself. We may feel frustrated that something we thought was gone for good, has come back.

It is helpful to realize that often our journey inward is a spiral one, not linear. We may be revisiting the same issue, but at a deeper level than before. This is so we can get closer and closer to our core, our essence. This is a gentle way to allow our new beliefs to really take hold in the real world. It is like having a frostbitten hand. If you plunge the hand immediately in hot water, damage will be done, because the capillaries have not had time to open up to allow the blood to flow properly. If the hand is placed first in cold water, then cool, then warm, and then hot water, the hand has time to gradually get accustomed to the changes.

TRADING FEAR FOR FREEDOM

Sometimes fear is caused, in the first place, by our being made to do things that do not fit for us. Fear also may be caused because we are trying to force something that we are not ready for at all levels. If we realized this, we would not try to force the fear out of ourselves. We could then give ourselves time to make the internal changes we need, so that fear will have nothing internally to cling to and will simply leave.

There is no set formula for releasing fear. Each person is unique. Even within us, fear will not be dealt with in the same way each time we have something come up. What may work for us at one time, may not be what is called for the next time. The information here is simply given as possible tools to use. You may find other things which work for you. Do not discount your way and do thank yourself for your creativity and cleverness.

Observe your fear

Become your own dispassionate, nonjudgmental observer. This means that you look at yourself from a higher place. Watch what is happening to you, the person, in the moment. Do not analyze or beat on yourself. Witness and internally take note of feelings, images, and thoughts which come to you.

From this higher vantage point, ask yourself what you are fearful of. You may need to probe to identify what the real issue is that represents fear to you. Remember that the probe is a gentle request for understanding, not an inquisition.

As the observer, pay attention to your body for clues that a real cause of the fear has been realized. There may be a tightening in your stomach, a lump in your throat, a desire to crawl under a blanket, a flood of tears, a desire to run from the room, or a sense of calm. Whatever the body reaction, your body will give you signs which help you through your fear process.

Use of intuition can be very helpful for the observer. Go in the direction your intuition draws you. It may suggest questions to ask the fearful part which will give clues to the real issue.

It may be helpful to ask, "What is the root cause of this fear?" or "What is the underlying cause of this fear?" As the observer, you may be surprised to find seemingly unrelated issues tied together in the fear. Do not assume that the fear will be rational, because it generally is not. When irrational pieces are brought to the surface, you will simply witness them, without judging whether they make sense, and record the information internally.

Feel the fear

Once the observer has assisted in finding out what the fear is about, it will be necessary for you to feel the fear deeply, to get rid of it. Most people stop here. They make a U-Turn out of themselves because they want to avoid feeling the full impact of the fear. If you do this, you will revert back into the dulled pain the fear has caused all along without the benefit of the resolution almost at hand.

Many people at this point commit to feeling the fear. But what they do when it starts to come to the surface is "think about feeling the fear." Thinking about fear seems safe because we can hide in our heads, with fear a *concept* rather than the actual feeling.

But the only way to feel the fear is to go beyond thinking about it, and dive directly into feeling it. You must muster all of the courage you can to experience the horror, anguish, and anger or whatever else may accompany the fear. You have to acknowledge the fear at a gut level. In that moment you may need to relive the past experience, or imagined ones. Whatever it takes to stay with the passion of your fear is what you must do so it can be released.

It might be helpful to remember that whatever caused your fear cannot really harm you in *this* moment of experiencing it. You are actually safe and alive. There is no real danger.

If you are not able to stay with the fear to release it, you may not be ready yet. Do not give yourself a hard time about it. You might need someone there with you like a partner, friend or therapist to be a supportive anchor for you in this process.

You'll want to reassure yourself that it is very scary to deal with fear. Give yourself credit for going as far as you did. Next time you reach for the root of the fear, you will probably be able to stretch yourself a little further, just because you were willing to go where you did the first time.

Nurture yourself

To permanently release fear around any issue requires that we nurture ourselves, to reassure the child part of us that it is okay to have whatever fear is there. Nurturing ourselves says, "I love you no matter what and I will be here for you." When you are in the midst of experiencing the fear fully as described above, it is particularly important for the nurturing part of you to be fully present to express love during the process.

We must be willing to nurture ourselves on a continuing basis for fear not to return. There are lots of ways to nurture ourselves. Taking a bubble bath, going for walks, cuddling our cat or dog, seeing a funny movie, playing a game, talking to a friend, reading a book, or giving ourselves a massage are some.

There are also some specific healing tools. The following have been used by many to help deal with fear as well as other issues in their lives:

Using affirmations

Affirmations can be very useful tools for releasing old fear tapes which have been with us for a long time. Affirmations can be especially helpful if we are not sure why the fear is present and are still trying to get to the root of it.

Affirmations also can be used to create new thought patterns not based on fear. To be most effective they should be stated in the positive. This is so that our mind focuses on what we want rather than what we don't want. They should also be stated in the present tense, so that our mind starts believing that we already are living without fear. Once our mind really believes this, it will help us to feel and act without fear. The following are some sample affirmations. These may be helpful to you, but the best ones will the ones you create to fit your specific needs:

1. I release the need to _____(e.g., suffer, be afraid of life, have love be hurtful, make things rough on myself).
2. I forgive myself for _____(e.g., needing to be a victim for all those years, hurting myself or others, not having life all figured out).
3. It is now safe for me to _____(e.g. be totally myself, speak up for myself, breathe deeply and fully through my body, relax).
4. With each day that passes, I feel safer and safer.
5. I now command out, all fear and doubt.
6. I now transform my fear into courage, excitement, and joy!

Use the mirror to rid ourselves of fear
When we were children, we freely soaked up the love others gave us because we knew that we deserved it. Because we are such innately wonderful beings, why wouldn't we deserve it?

As we grew up and began to forget that we were wonderful, we may have also stopped allowing ourselves to receive love. As adults, only we can decide how much love we will allow in. If we haven't allowed in much love, we will probably start to feel fearful. But we can turn around this downward spiral of fear.

One technique we can use is to look at ourselves in the mirror and send ourselves love. By doing this, we are affirming that we unconditionally love the person we see looking back at us.

Some people have difficulty looking at themselves in this way. When I began mirror work, I felt embarrassed to do it. I thought I might be being narcissistic to look at myself. But I looked anyway. I found that I attacked myself and saw only flaws. But by continuing to look and send love no matter what verbal attacks came out, I found that over time the fear started to dissipate. More and more love started coming through as the attacks lessened and eventually stopped.

It has been very healing for me to look at myself. Now when I look into my eyes, I feel that I see straight to my essence. Now I know what is there and I have less fear about the world around me.

This may be a useful technique for you. You may want to try it and see what happens.

Imagery
The use of imagery can be a very powerful tool to release fear and heal old fear wounds.

Imagery has an artistry to it which goes *beyond mere thinking* about the fear. It provides the *experience* of fear.

Images may come to you from dreams, past experiences, fantasies, books, friends, movies, or any other source you choose. Since they are your own creation, you can use imagery anyway you want to help.

When you use imagery, nothing is taboo as long as you are able to separate the fact from the fantasy. For instance, when dealing with the angry fear of a particular person, I found myself wanting to kill that person. Because of the taboo against killing, I refused to let myself have that image. After several weeks, it would come up again. Then one day my inner voice said, "Go ahead and do it. You won't really hurt the person. You are only *imagining* that you are doing it." As soon as I gave myself permission to have the image clearly in my mind, the fearful and angry feelings began to tumble out. The full force of feelings lasted about 2 minutes and then it was over. Because I used the image, I was able to release the fear which had been trapped within me. What had been with me for so long was totally gone. It was gone because I was able to use imagery as a powerful healing tool.

Transforming anger into a real strength

As I deal with my own issues about anger, I have discovered that I have a constant underlying theme beneath the presenting situation. It is there whether I am angry toward an injustice in the world, others, or myself. The theme is: "I feel like a victim who is not going to get to fulfill my life's purpose or be who I am capable of being." On the surface, I may feel angry toward a boss, parent, partner or someone else. But this is only because I am perceiving at the moment that the other person is standing in my way. I may be angry toward myself because I find that I get in my own way, like a small puppy with large, ungainly feet.

Now when I begin to feel angry, I ask myself, "Where am I feeling like a victim? Who or what is standing in my way? What do I need to know or do in this situation?" I listen to my answer.

Often the person or situation is giving me a valuable lesson which I find I am resistant to learn. I then confront my resistance and ask *truthfully* what this person is trying to teach me. When I am told what the lesson is, I review where there have been similar situations in interactions with others. If there is a pattern, I may become even angrier, temporarily. When I see my anger increasing, I know I am about to reach the "motherlode core" issue. But at this point, I am generally angry because I have to admit that it is a pattern which I was responsible for creating. Owning my responsibility is the beginning of the internal change process, to rid the pattern at the root of my anger.

Sometimes when a pattern becomes clear, I also have anger toward myself for feeling so stupid that I didn't see the pattern when it was there all the time. Now I forgive myself and say, "Oh, well. At least I see it now." This helps me release my anger by feeling the emotions underneath the anger. As my healing progresses, I am able to thank the person or situation for pushing me to learn something I needed to know.

Sometimes I look within and don't see a lesson for myself from the other person. When this is the case, I accept that maybe I am being someone else's lesson. I then release any "hooks" that I have allowed to be placed in me from the other person's anger. Instead of wasting any of my energy becoming angry back at the other person, I consciously channel that energy back into constructive areas of my life. I say such affirmations as, "No one can hurt me with their anger (or keep me from being me, keep me from doing what I want with my life, divert my attention away from my truth, etc.)." I repeat the words while I feel the anger energy transform into strength from my core, pushing out the victim energy and radiating strong energy into the space around me. After doing this, I check internally to find out if there is any anger remaining that needs to be addressed. If there is, I usually feel more ready to hear the new message, because I have affirmed my strength.

Finding the balance point can make anger a strength instead of an energy zapper. This is an internal process that you must explore for yourself. Only you know your internal terrain and the part anger plays in your being strong. I present my process because it was a turning point in my not letting myself be victimized by anger. Anger can divert my attention away from being happy if I let it. It happens less frequently as I continue to practice this technique. I now see my anger as a tool which helps propel me toward self-discovery and personal fulfillment.

Turning hurt into love

Feeling hurt is a choice. We can allow verbal or physical barbs to penetrate our boundaries and emotionally puncture our essence, or we can pull the barbs out of us and throw them away. We can also change the emotion attached to the barb or decide that we need have no emotion attached to someone else's barb.

We have the ability, to change hurt in midstream to joy. When we are able to use our emotions in this way, we are able to feel strong and proud of ourselves. We have protected ourselves and set things into motion for changing internal patterns which have previously damaged us.

We can detach from feeling hurt when we realize that it is someone else's way of lashing out in hurt and doesn't have to be anything for us. This frees us to have love and compassion for the other person because our emotional energy is not occupied in feeling hurt. We can realize that others only throw barbs our way to distance themselves for their own protection.

Release

After you are able to feel the fear deeply, an important part of the process is to release the fear. Some people skip this step. When the fear comes back to them in another form, they don't understand why. They think that the process didn't work. But actually, the release is essential for us to go on with our lives.

Even if we have not liked living with fear, when it is gone, we will need to grieve as part of the releasing process. It has been with us so long that we will need to say goodbye. This is letting go of the old to usher in the new.

To let go also means that we must forgive ourselves and others for causing the fear to be with us. If we still harbor anger at ourselves or others about what happened in the past, we only hurt ourselves and keep ourselves tied to the fear.

Releasing can be a very soothing feeling. A parent picks up a child and loves it to offer comfort and reassurance after a fright. Releasing fear is our way of loving and offering comfort to ourselves.

Make room for freedom to enter

When a long held fear is released, you may sense a void because you have had so much energy tied up in keeping the fear down. (You also may have extra unexplained energy while you are getting used to your new-found freedom.) Accept the void as part of the process. To be filled with something new requires that you first empty out the old.

During this time it is the perfect opportunity to create a new reality for yourself which does not have fear as its basis. You may find new affirmations which are lighter and more joyful. New images may spontaneously come to you. And you may find that former beliefs are now transformed into knowledge.

Allow yourself to savor your changes. Reward yourself. Give yourself lots of positive strokes. You deserve it! You have shown yourself that *you are your own best friend.*

When We Release Fear, Our Body Shows It

Some of the specific body ailments listed earlier take time to cure or reverse themselves after we have eliminated fear. But there are ways that our body may tell us immediately that we have gotten rid of core fear issues. Below is a list of some of the body signs experienced by myself and others:

1. Pores of the skin open
2. Feelings of being physically much lighter
3. Toxins released into the bladder to be expelled
4. Awareness heightened, including:
   a. Sight sharpened
   b. Smells more aromatic
   c. Hearing more acute
   d. Intuition enhanced

e. Clearer thinking
f. Touch more sensuous
5. More grounded. Body feels more connected to earth
6. Breathing deepens and is relaxed
7. Increased circulation to hands and feet
8. Tension released in neck, shoulders, back, diaphragm
9. Less anxiety and nervousness
10.More laughter

Fear as a Habit

Because fear may have been with us for so long, it may have become a habit. Even though we may have felt like we have shed the cause of the fear, our internal feelings and our external behavior may still appear as if we are afraid.

For instance, suppose there has been an internal fear which has caused you to hunch your shoulders for many years. Even though you have gotten to the root of the fear, you may still find yourself hunching your shoulders without realizing it. In a nonjudgmental way you may need to remind yourself that the reason for the fear is no longer there and so it is okay to relax your shoulders. Habits take a long time to form, so we need to allow ourselves time to rid ourselves of them.

CHAPTER 12
Embracing Courage

*"Everyday living requires courage if life
is to be effective and bring happiness."*
Maxwell Maltz

To live without a mask requires that we be willing to be courageous. While the mask encourages us to play many games, one of the few that it doesn't want us to play is the game of "How Courageous Can I Be?"

The mask knows that if we draw upon our courage, we will no longer be willing to play the "games of the mask." When we are courageous, we are not easy to control. Courage pumps up our energy so we *know* that our dreams are achievable. Nothing and no one can hold us back. The "games of the mask" seen through the eyes of courage seem silly, hollow, and without meaning. Courage shows the mask for what it really is; a symbol of tyranny.

Be Willing to Take Risks

To be courageous, we have to take risks. We must be willing to give up the familiar, the status quo, to stretch ourselves to new heights.

Risk-taking is the natural way that our essence urges us toward fulfillment and toward enjoyment of life. Without risk-taking, we become stagnant and unenthusiastic about life. We become like robots going routinely through the motions without experiencing anything.

Risk-taking challenges us to push outside of our "safety zone," so that we can open to a new level of understanding and awareness. Once we have gone outside our known territory, our "safety zone" increases to a new level. We now have less fear of the world around us. We are able to devote our energy to love and fulfillment rather than protection and survival.

Learn the Lessons from "Mistakes"

When faced with taking risks, we may think that there is a chance we can harm ourselves by extending ourselves or choosing incorrectly. This view of risk-taking implies that we can fail by making an "incorrect" choice. If we begin to understand that there are no mistakes in life, then we will know that there are no "incorrect" choices. There are only opportunities to learn about ourselves, those around us, and the nature of the world. Choosing this view helps us to rise to the challenges life presents us, learn the lesson, and move on.

An example of this is: If Jill has a hard time with responsibility about money, situations will continue to come up where she is offered the chance to be responsible. Jill can choose to ignore the lessons and just *say* she is "naturally" irresponsible or she can do something about it. Once she really has learned to be financially responsible, she can move on to other lessons.

So, risk-taking is a mindset. We can choose to see making decisions as potentials for mistakes and ways to hurt ourselves. Or, we can see risk-taking as an adventure to learn and have fun.

See the "hologram" of your life
It is sometimes so easy to see what other people are doing to themselves to create their victim roles. But it is sometimes harder for us to see ourselves and the victim roles we play, because we are right in the middle of them.

When we step back and see our lives as if we were watching a hologram of ourselves, we will get a different perspective than from inside ourselves. Looking at ourselves in this way allows us to see ourselves as others see us. We are able to release the belief that things "happen to us." As we have discussed earlier, this attitude makes us victims. Life falls on us like "a load of bricks." We see it as our "chore" to uncover ourselves from the pile of rubble.

When we see the hologram that our life is, we can see patterns emerge which make our lives unique. But to appreciate this uniqueness, we must rise above the day to day minutia which occupies most of our thoughts.

If we look at our lives as if we were reading a best-selling novel about ourselves, we will see that it is full of drama, tragedy, intrigue, romance and suspense. We are our own heroes and heroines. Appreciating our own unfolding life in this way makes it difficult to put our book down. We want to become a part of it more fully. We realize that we are not only the reader, but the writer of this fascinating story. We can choose if the story has a dull, lifeless ending or an exciting, fun filled grand finale.

Release perfection and judgment

It is much easier for us to take risks when we give up our need to be perfect. Perfection is something the mask sets up for us to strive toward, but never achieve. It is a sure-fire way for us to feel like failures. It keeps us from just enjoying who we are and who we are becoming.

As we release perfection, we lose the need to be judgmental about our "mistakes." We stop seeing our errors as tragedies. We stop beating on ourselves internally for not knowing or not having done it "right." We simply learn from the specific situations, thank ourselves for seeing the situation differently now, and move on.

"Mistakes" reprogrammed into "lessons"

We can reprogram our way of thinking about "mistakes" by doing some very simple things. When a situation occurs which we feel was a "mistake," we can ask ourselves questions which will turn the experience into a learning opportunity. Here are some sample questions you may want to ask yourself:

1. Did I operate from my external programming, or did I come from my truth?
2. Did I listen to my intuition before I listened to my logic?

3. Did I *respond* to the situation from essence, or did I *react* from circumstances outside of myself?
4. Did I act from fear and protection, or from love and expansion?
5. Did I stay true to my personal integrity?
6. Were there obvious signs that I did not pay attention to?
7. Were there signs that I saw, but chose to override?
8. Were there pieces of information I was missing, before the incident that I now have access to?
9. Did I rigidly hold onto old outdated views of reality which do not fit anymore?
10. If the situation arises again, what would I do differently?
11. Is there a pattern for me in my response which I can learn from?
12. Am I being gentle with myself about this situation?

If you become aware of your part in situations that arise, you will better be able to turn your "mistakes" into "lessons." With practice, you will be able to ask yourself useful questions while you are in the middle of the situation. Sometimes you change the outcome just by awareness. Later you will be able to start asking yourself these questions before situations arise. You will be able to play them out in advance and decide if you want to go ahead with this situation or do something else instead.

Release the experience, hold onto the lesson

An important aspect in transforming "mistakes" into "lessons" is to release the experience after it is over. You don't have to replay it repeatedly to remember it. Repeating it too often will do more harm than good because it will feel like you are beating yourself up. You will always have access to the information in your internal memory bank any time you need it. Releasing it in your conscious awareness simply allows you internal space for new experiences and new lessons.

Learning lessons is not linear

It is important to be aware that our learning is not linear. Just because we got something one time, does not mean that we may not fall back into old patterns, or forget what we learned. It may take time for the new lessons to become as permanently ingrained as the old way of doing things.

Understanding that our learning is not smooth can help us to be gentler on ourselves. Especially when we are in the midst of doing things we thought we had already changed. I had a therapist who used to remind me, *"5 steps forward, 3 steps back."*

So, if you find yourself acting in old ways, honor those experiences as well as the new ones. There is a difference now. You are acting from more awareness, so the old experiences probably do not feel as comfortable as they once did. It is like wearing a new pair of shoes. At first they are not as comfortable as the old shoes. But after you have worn them awhile and step back into the old shoes, they no longer feel as good as they once did. Your feet have changed and the old shoes no longer fit the "new" you. But you don't realize how good your new fit is unless you have something to compare it to.

Develop a "Courage Power Pack"

Presented here is an image which has aided me to feel more courageous. I hope that it may be useful for you as well.

I imagined a T.V. commercial with a man fumbling around in his closet looking for something. He pulls out what appears to be a backpack and he puts it on his back. He says, "I used to be scared all of the time until I started carrying my "courage power pack" with me wherever I go." Words would flash up on the screen, as we hear Karl Malden saying, "Courage: Don't leave home without it."

The "courage power pack" idea first came to me when I saw a preview for the movie, "Rocketeers." I had been dealing with my own issues about courage that day. When I saw the rocket on the main character's back, I thought, "Now that's what I need. But instead of rocket fuel, I want mine to have courage." After that I set about developing my own "courage power pack."

I went to my internal laboratory and started gathering materials to put in my pack. I chose the following items:

1. All past experiences in which I exhibited courage, even in a small way.
2. The words of confidence I heard from my internal parent saying:
   a. "You can do it; I have faith in you."
   b. "I am proud of you."
3. My affirmations:
   a. "If someone says it can't be done, I will translate it as a, YES I CAN."
   b. "No one and nothing can keep me from being courageous!"
4. All of the tools and techniques I have acquired about getting rid of fear.
5. An image of myself being courageous and strong, yet gentle and loving.
6. Memory of what it feels like in my body when I am courageous.

Since developing my "courage power pack," I have found that when I need a dose of courage, I now have this image to turn to. It brings together all of the other images, thoughts, and feelings which represent my individual courage. I actually feel like I strap on my "courage power pack" and soak up the courage it emits. It gives me support when I need it. And it gives me a little jet-propelled uplift to meet whatever challenges present themselves to me.

Become Self-Disciplined

Self-discipline is often what sets apart those who get what they want from those who do not. When people look upon someone who has "made it," they just see the end result and may not realize that self-discipline played an important role in shaping that person into who he or she is. If you ask those who feel successful, what they attribute their success to, many will say it is self-discipline. This one aspect kept them going when all others said something couldn't be done, or their prospects to do it looked bleak. What sets these people apart is that they kept their focus and just did what was needed to achieve their goals.

We may try something new for awhile. When it doesn't get immediate results, without self-discipline we will likely fall back into old patterns which sabotage ourselves. Without self-discipline we may use this as justification for continuing to feel like victims. Like a good victim we can say, "I tried it, but it just didn't work out." Many people use this as their victim motto through life. They refuse to admit that the very lack of self-discipline is what keeps them from breaking free from the victim role.

Self-discipline is a choice. We can choose to look at our difficult issues, or go to a movie. We can practice our gymnastic moves all summer, to prepare for competition, or we can hang around the mall with friends and shop. We can choose to deal with our spouse about a problem, or use avoidance by going to a bar after work. We can choose to complain to our friends about our weight, or we can change our image of ourselves by getting professional help, exercising more, and/or eating less.

There is no set formula which makes for discipline, but here are some things you can do to keep yourself on track so you don't slip back into old bad habits while you strengthen your courage to stay focused.

1. When you are clear about your desires or goals and really get excited about them, make a list of what you will need to do to stay on track. Refer back to the list when you are at a low point or can't remember what you need to do to meet your goals.

2. Keep a journal which specifically helps you to see the lessons and patterns in your life. When you make a "mistake," look back at what you have already learned to see if the new situation fits. Does it give you a new piece of your puzzle to figure out?

3. If you see yourself doing things in the old pattern, ask yourself, "Do I really want to do this? Or am I avoiding doing what I know will help me to get what I want?"

   Example: You feel that you want to look for a new job, but say to yourself that you need to update your resume. When you have time to work on your resume, do you instead clean out a closet, update your address book, or find other tasks which you have "needed to do" for a year?

4. If you decide to do the thing that you believe interferes with what you really want to do, notice

if you enjoy it. Are you operating on automatic pilot or is it as necessary or fun as you thought?
Example: You want to compose a song, but instead you go to the refrigerator and eat some ice cream. Eat the ice cream with awareness. Does it taste really good? Is that what you really wanted? Does eating the ice cream make you feel good or do you feel guilty and angry with yourself?

5. If you are stuck in a routine which seems to make it hard for you to do what you want to do, vary your routine.
Example: You want to exercise more. You wake up in the mornings resolving that today after work, you will exercise. But after work you are tired and hungry. Instead of exercising you collapse with a T.V. dinner in front of the television. Change your routine by exercising in the morning before you are awake enough to talk yourself out of it.

6. If you want to do something, but there never seems to be enough time to get to it, set specific time aside for yourself.
Example: You want to write a children's book. Let everyone in the family know you will be unavailable from 8:00-9:00 PM. Do not do anything else during this time. If family or friends interrupt you, firmly remind them that this is your uninterrupted time and you will be available after nine.

Be Willing to Stand Alone in Your Truth

One very important aspect of courage is our willingness to stand alone in our truth. It is easy to feel courageous when we are surrounded by others who are saying or doing the same thing that we are. But this is false courage. The truly courageous are willing to stick with their truth no matter how few others agree with them or back them. Mahatma Gandhi who knew real courage said it well,

"Strength in numbers is the delight of the timid. The valiant in spirit glory in fighting alone."

Truth is something that cannot be voted on. There can be, and often has been, mass delusion. Otherwise, tyrants would never be able to run over people in wholesale lots. If our truth tells us the opposite of what everyone else around us says, we will exhibit true courage by refusing to go along with others.

Standing alone in our truth will take real dedication at times. We may be tested by situations to see how far we are willing to go, to back our truth. Are we willing to face the perceived risk of losing a job, our spouse, or the love of our parents by stating our truth?

Often we may find that standing with our truth does not bring the actual consequences we feared. The fear was only a way to mask our truth. Once we are truthful, we are then free from the bondage of fear. We may not actually lose the job, spouse, or parental love by stating the truth.

If we lose those things, the lesson is *not*, "we should not have told the truth." The lesson may be to see if we will *abandon our truth* to get something from others. The lesson also might be that we need to let go of the job, spouse, or need for parental love. We can then allow others into our lives who may better fit our level of truth, integrity, and love.

Many people fear that they will be lonely if they stand in their truth. This may be the case in the short run. If we are truly courageous, we will allow ourselves to experience short-term loneliness, for long-term gain. There may be a need to empty the people out of our lives who we have outgrown. This is necessary before we can replace them with others who better match our new level of commitment to ourselves.

If we continue to stay with our truth, we will begin to realize we are never really alone. We have *ourselves.*

Embracing Our Courage
May Mean Asking for Help

Being willing to stand alone in our truth does not mean that we have to heal in isolation. Sometimes the courageous thing to do is ask for help. This may be from friends, a therapist, or perhaps a sponsor in a 12-step program.

Getting support is not the same as leaning on others. When we lean on others, we are asking them to prop us up. We are still denying our responsibility to heal ourselves. **When we ask for support, we ask others to help prop *ourselves* up.** The outward appearance may be very difficult to distinguish but the internal shift in perception is enormous. Asking for support is acknowledging to ourselves that with a helping hand we are capable of freeing ourselves from our own victimization.

Don't Take Life Too Seriously

As mentioned earlier, risk-taking is easier to do if we see life as an adventure, instead of a series of mistakes. To see life this way, we have to lighten up and not take life or the people around us too seriously.

One of the reasons we have looked at the "games of the mask" and masks we wear in the way that we have, is to see the funny side of human nature. So often, when we are in the middle of dealing with challenges, we take them too seriously. We miss the fact that others are just seeing whether we will play the game with them. When we understand this then we can say to ourselves, "I see the game, but no thanks."

Strengthening our courage does not have to be a stressful, heavy process. In fact, as we lighten up, we invite in courage. After awhile there is a snowball effect. The more courage we have, the more courage we are likely to let in. And feeling more courageous allows us to feel strong and capable of fulfilling our dreams and enjoying being just who we now are.

CHAPTER 13

Ditching the Struggle

*"Life was never meant to be a struggle;
just a gentle progression from one point
to another, much like walking through a
valley on a sunny day."*
Stuart Wilde

What is Struggle?

We all know when life feels like a struggle. Struggle to get up in the morning. Struggle with projects at work. Struggle with our family members. But what exactly is this thing that sometimes feels like it has a life of its own inside of us?

Struggle is defined in the dictionary as, "To make one's way with difficulty, violent exertion." Struggle implies hardship and turmoil. There is often judgment which goes along with struggle.

As with so many other things we have looked at, there is an opposite side of the coin for struggle. Otherwise, there would be nothing for the struggle to push against. So what is the opposite of struggle? Ease and freedom from difficulty.

Ease and struggle have one element in common; they both require effort. Effort is the use of energy to get something done by exertion of strength or mental power. But there is no judgment in effort for it is not easy or a struggle. There is effort for a seed to push out of the ground to become a flower. But it doesn't say, "Boy, did I have a tough time blooming." Neither does it say, "It was easier than I thought to become a flower." The plant just grows and blooms into a flower with an effort that was neither easy nor difficult as far as the plant was concerned; it just did it.

Struggle is not a natural thing. It is something that we clever humans manufacture for ourselves. **Struggle is effort to which we have attached negative emotions and desperation.** The mask encourages us to play the "game of struggle" because it makes us easier to control if we think that life is difficult. We are more willing to do things someone else's way, if we feel that life is difficult no matter how we do it.

But just as we can attach negative emotions to effort, we can also choose to assign positive emotions to it so we no longer feel like we are struggling. This is what "ditching the struggle" is about. It is changing our internal perception about where we choose to exert our strength and mental power, so that we can flow with ease through life.

Why Ditch the Struggle?

The main reason to let go of struggle is because it doesn't feel good. It doesn't feel good emotionally and it doesn't feel good in our body.

Emotionally, struggle keeps us feeling desperate. We stay perpetually feeling hopeless within our difficulties. We become like a thirsty person wandering in the desert in search of water. Maybe we'll stumble upon what we want to quench our need, but we feel that the chance of finding our oasis is slim.

Struggle keeps us emotionally tied in knots. Our energy is kept wrapped around itself in an internal battle. This means that we have very little available energy for anything else, like having fun.

Struggle without resolving the emotions involved, can start to affect our body. Tension can be felt almost immediately as one of the first signs that we are in the midst of struggle. Shoulder tension is one of the most common indicators that we are "carrying the burden" of struggle. If we continue to struggle for any length of time, we may start to have aches, pains, hyperactivity, or fatigue. All of these can be an indication that we are spending an excessive amount of energy, like Sisyphus, continuing to unsuccessfully roll our stone of struggle up the hill. If we don't pay attention to these signs, then our body may have to wave a flag in front of us. This may result in an ulcer or heart attack to get our attention and alert us to how the struggle is hurting to us.

Struggle is Championed as a Virtue

We have been around struggle so long, we consider it a virtue. We see it as an object like the flag to rally round. Rather than dealing with why we struggle, and doing something about it, we get together and compare notes on how we have each struggled in our lives, as if this justifies our existence. We pat one another on the back and say, "There, there. What a good little struggler you are." This creates a group of people who reward each other and perpetuate each other's struggle.

Mistaking Struggle for Excitement

There are some people who are addicted to struggle because they mistake struggle for life's excitement. They see their struggle as a drama which has interesting twists and turns. Soap operas would not be as popular, if there wasn't confusion between struggle and excitement.

When we talk in terms of things being easy, many people will equate in their minds, "Easy = Boring." But this is only an illusion to keep the struggle alive. Life can be easy *and* exciting at the same time.

We cannot experience *true excitement* about life until we quit struggling. That true excitement is pure bliss. Bliss is felt at a more profound level than the emotions, thoughts, or body alone. It is a *total being* experience, which cannot be adequately described in words. Once you have experienced bliss, you will know that struggle is only a way to keep us addicted to a poor substitute for what we are really looking for.

Why do We Choose Struggle?

We are taught how to struggle from the time we are tiny tots. We received messages all through our growing up like, "Life is a struggle," "If you want anything in life you have to struggle for it," "It's not worth as much, if you didn't struggle for it." Or, "Those who work hard are rewarded in heaven." We heard adults say, "I am struggling with that issue," "I've wrestled the problem to the ground," etc.

We also were rewarded (or promised rewards) for struggling. When we were children, we may have been rewarded with an extra allowance if we would do something we found particularly distasteful, like cleaning out the gutters. At work, we see the workaholics who stay until 10:00 PM every night on a project get the available raises or promotions. Governments tell their citizens, "If you tighten your belt just a little bit more, we will get through this economic crisis and you will get what you want."

Many people struggle because they don't know another way to approach life. Struggle has been so ingrained that they operate on automatic pilot, never stopping to see or feel what they are doing. The momentum of going forward in struggle may engulf their energy completely. Even if an easy way to do something is handed to these people on a silver platter, it will be rejected, without a second thought.

This is because they are so enmeshed in the struggle mentality. Some people may decide they don't want to struggle and stop doing it for awhile. Then they get negative pressure from others who are still struggling. So they succumb to the pressure and get back into the struggle attempting to roll their stones up the hill along with everyone else. To justify going back to the struggle, they may say, "I tried to make things easy, but that's just not the way life is." They chose not to see that they faced an internal test. That test was to see if they really were ready to give up the struggle. For many, the answer was that they were not.

Releasing Struggle
Through Internal Change

When we look at other people struggling through life, we often see that they are creating more struggle than is necessary in a given situation. It is so much easier to see struggle in other people. But when we are in the middle of our own struggle, we often have difficulty understanding what we are doing to create it. We think that outside influences are conspiring against us to make things difficult.

Sometimes we continue to experience life as a struggle because we have not yet created the right conditions internally to release the struggle. It is impossible for non-struggling energy to come in, unless we make room for it by getting rid of some of the struggle energy.

How we view struggle

Maybe we still believe internally that struggle is a virtue. If this is the case, no amount of external action will create anything but struggle, because our internal and external realities do not match. We may not have given up the belief that excitement is derived from the struggle. If we still believe this, we will not give up the struggle, because as human beings we have a need for life to be exciting.

Examination of our goals

We may not be disciplined enough to reach our goals. We say that we want something and may really believe it, but our attention and energy wanders, and does not stay focused clearly on the goal. An example of this would be working on a project. We start to outline how the project is to get done and then we get sidetracked. We may start to think about another spin-off project. Without discipline to pull us back to the main focus, we can create struggle for ourselves to complete the original project.

There may be times when we have lots of goals and are struggling to get all of these goals met. This may be because we are trying to do too many things at once, which dilutes our effort.

We may also need to examine our goals to see if they are realistic, or if we are setting ourselves up for a struggle. Sometimes things take longer to bring into reality, because we think faster than we are able to act. When we try to stick to unrealistic goals, we also create an unnecessary burden of struggle for ourselves.

Need for acceptance

If we need to be accepted by others, chances are that we will be strugglers. Need for acceptance leads us into doing things other people's way rather than our own. Struggle is inevitably created when we do things everyone else's way but our own. It is likely that the very people we crave acceptance from are also strugglers. They will stroke us for struggling and reject us if we choose not to struggle. When we want acceptance from others, we also are leaving ourselves open to allowing them to control us. This will always create an internal struggle, as we try to shake loose from their grip.

Ability to listen to our truth

Struggle will also be present within us when we listen to what the particular mask we are wearing tells us to do, rather than listening to our truth. This is because we create difficulty for ourselves by having part of us going in one direction and part of us wanting to go in another. We are like the Siamese twins when one wanted to turn to the left and the other wanted to turn to the right.

Need for balance

If we are still struggling, it is because we lack balance and stability in some aspect of our life. If we want to release struggle, we have to continue to clear obstacles out of our way. It may take time to recreate ease in our lives. As things in our life get easy on one level, we need to make sure that we don't inadvertently replace one struggle for another. Otherwise, we will still be out of balance.

The best strugglers may create the ultimate struggle. That is "struggling to ditch the struggle." If we see ourselves trying too hard to get rid of struggle, it is a sure sign we have not yet learned how to live a life of balance.

Changing From Struggle to Ease

The difference between struggle and ease is the difference between living life from the outside in, or the inside out. With struggle, we are reacting to situations, people and events outside ourselves. We have to disconnect from ourselves to put our energy "out there." When we live with ease, the same things may be going on externally, but we radiate our energy outward from our essence. Since the energy comes from a natural place, there is nothing for the energy to struggle against.

This internal shift in perception is what makes something easy, instead of a struggle. It is not that we necessarily change the events around us, but that we change our *perception* about the events. Once we change our perception, then events around us may also change, but that is not our goal. Part of letting go of the struggle is letting go of the need to control things "out there" and instead focus our attention inside ourselves to what is "in here."

Struggle's Challenge to Us

Whenever there is struggle, there is a gift of a lesson we need to know. If we ignore the message, then it is likely the struggle will increase. We can either burn out, or listen to and act on the message. If we see struggle as a useful tool which challenges us to examine ourselves, then we will have received the gift.

Are we loving ourselves?

Struggle may be telling us that we are not really showing love for ourselves. We may be using struggle as a way to punish ourselves for being bad, mean, or unlovable. We may not have forgiven ourselves for something in the past. If this is so, we are using struggle as our penance.

Are we going at our natural pace?

Are we dancing to someone else's drummer? Chances are that if there is struggle, we are not going at our natural pace. We may need to slow down or we may need to speed up. But whatever the pace, it will be different than the pace of the struggle.

DITCHING THE STRUGGLE

Is there an easier way?
Sometimes we are so involved in the struggle that we do not see easier ways of doing things. The struggle may be pushing so hard that we must stop to get our breath. During the break, we may be able to see that an easier way has presented itself involving no struggle.

Do we need to let go of something?
There are times when the struggle is trying to tell us that we are not doing what we really want to be doing. It may not be what will make us happy or fulfilled. Struggle sometimes offers us the opportunity to reevaluate what really fits for us and to let go of what doesn't.

Do we need to change our attitude?
Struggle sometimes is telling us that we need to change our attitude rather than what we are doing. We may be doing something which we do not like to do, but is a necessary part of our growth or training. We may be doing it so that later we will have all the pieces we need to carry out our purpose in life. The struggle may be like the "Karate Kid" having to paint the fence and wax the car. He did not understand at the time why he had to do those things. When his teacher later showed him karate moves, he saw that they related to the earlier tasks he had struggled with.

Do we need to clarify that nothing will deter us from our goal?

Struggle can be a test to see if we really want what we say we want. It pushes us to examine our priorities and issues. Struggle may show us that we really want something else.

It can also challenge us to see if we are ready to do what we want to do. If we crumble in the midst of struggle, it may show us that we need more preparation first.

Struggle challenges our resolve. If we are clear that what we are doing comes from a natural place within, struggle can make us stronger. Struggle may be our test to solidify our knowing that *nothing* will deter us from what we want.

Are we enjoying life?

For some, struggle feels like a very grim game and one which must be played seriously. We may be *working at life* and not allowing what we do to flow, be fun, and childlike. If we are finding very little joy in life, struggle may be trying to tell us that we need to do other things which will offer us more happiness.

How do We Ditch the Struggle?

Getting rid of the struggle begins with a choice. We must decide we are tired of the "game of struggle" and want to ditch it. We must be willing to stop seeing struggle as something outside of us and be willing to face it squarely as our issue. And we have to commit ourselves to do whatever it takes to lessen or completely rid ourselves of the struggle.

Become aware that we are struggling
The first step to getting rid of struggle is to see that we are struggling. This means that we must rise out of the middle of the struggle and once again become our own impartial observer. The observer does not judge the struggle or analyze why the struggle developed. *It only observes the behavior.*

This means that we observe how struggle effects our emotions. Do we stay constantly angry with ourselves or others? Do we feel a sense of futility about life? Do we feel anxious?

We can also observe how the struggle affects our body. Do we feel tightness in our neck, back, or buttocks? Do we clench our jaws? Does our whole body feel like a spring wound too tight? Do we have a knot in our stomach?

Our observation should include watching our actions from the outside. Do we see how we make things more difficult than they need to be? Do we move continually? Do we get easily upset when things don't turn out the way we planned?

Do we do any of the following flashing neon signs to indicate struggle?
1. We do the unnecessary things first, leaving the important ones for crunch time.
2. We do the horrible tasks first, leaving the fun ones to the end and then never get to them.

3. We have a clear idea what we need to do, but do what others tell us to do instead.
4. We sabotage ourselves by doing everything but the thing that needs to be done.
5. We count on someone else to help us in the struggle and then find we are left to do it by ourselves.

Be willing to examine ourselves

Deciding to ditch struggle is not an overnight process. If it were, we would probably have done away with it long ago. It is necessary to allow ourselves time to unravel what we have, for so long, woven into our way of dealing with life.

We may not like what we see at first when we realize why we have held onto the struggle for so long. But if we persevere, we will ultimately get down to our truth and essence. This awareness is what will end the struggle for us.

This process may require that we examine ourselves many times. If we commit to looking at our issues as often as necessary, we will be a long way on the road to moving beyond struggle.

1. Examining our feelings of worthiness

Much of our need to hang on to struggle has to do with our not feeling worthy of having it easy. We may feel like we are not as worthy as someone else we respect who is still struggling. We may feel that we don't deserve to be here in the first place, so we must struggle as a way to prove our worthiness. We may not feel like we are worthy of having things the way we want them because we didn't "work hard enough" for them. There may be other worthiness issues besides these that are uniquely yours. Whenever you see yourself struggling it may be a good idea to ask yourself if you have some worthiness issues.

2. **Do we care too much about what others think of us?**

This question goes back to our need for outside approval. Struggling often indicates that we want to please others. So we do things the way we imagine that they want us to do them. We need to ask ourselves, "Am I doing this because I am afraid of being disliked or because of peer pressure? Or am I doing this because *I* really want to do it."

3. **Do we think that our desires are unattainable?**

Do we believe that it is impossible to have things easy or the way we want them? If we don't believe we can have what we want, we won't let ourselves have it, even if it is within our reach. Sometimes we will not let go of the struggle. If we did, it might prove that the struggle was a lie of the mask's which we bought into. Because we don't want to admit that we were duped by the mask, we would rather keep our desires out of reach. The struggle can then stay alive without challenge.

SHEDDING THE LAYERS OF THE MASK

In her book, *Prospering Woman*, Ruth Ross, Ph.D., talks about women having a fear of success. But what she says applies for men as well as women, and for struggle, as well as success:

"Fear of success has sometimes been called the fear of the sublime–the fear of acknowledging that we really are great and wonderful beings. That idea is more than many of us can stand. Being prosperous [*or having things easy*] comes too close to proving it true."*

When we are willing to admit it to ourselves, fear of the sublime is what creates the struggle, within many of us, and holds us back from getting what we truly want in all areas of our lives.

Be willing to change old habits
When we have been struggling for a long period of time, it begins to become habit. Most of you have gone through the process of changing habits. You know that can be a struggle, if you aren't ready to let go of the habit. Described here are some of the ways you can start to break the habit of struggle:
1. When you see that you have struggled, think of how you could have done it differently to not have created the struggle. This does not mean that you should internally flog yourself for not having seen how to do it more easily. This

* Ruth Ross, *Prospering Woman* (Berkley: Whatever Publications, 1982), p. 46.

process is a nonjudgmental one. It requires that you bring in your impartial observer to simply state the facts as to how it could have been done more easily.

2. Be willing to let go of struggle without guilt. This becomes easier to do once you determine that the struggle is not trying to tell you something else. Remember, guilt is something that the mask wants you to hang onto to continue doing the mask's bidding. Picture the guilt going into the sky in a helium balloon until it is out of sight. When your desire to struggle is gone, and the guilt leaves, there is nothing for new struggle to cling to inside of you.

3. You may have a good idea, but the timing is off. Maybe you or others are not ready for it. Keep the idea on a back burner and ask if there are other things which need to be done first. Having the idea on a back burner frees you to carry through with new ideas whose timing may be more appropriate.

4. If you find yourself in the midst of struggle, start stepping back and look at yourself struggling. Be willing to change the way you are doing things in midstream, if that is what your truth tells you to do.

5. Before starting to do something, ask what is the easiest way it can be done. Then do it the easy way and completely avoid the struggle.

SHEDDING THE LAYERS OF THE MASK

Be willing to change our opinions about life

Since all of life involves change, it is really no big deal to change our opinion about life. Change opens us to new possibilities and expanded options for how to do things.

We only feel bad about changing our mind when we believe the lies of the mask. It wants us to believe that only the mask can decide when change happens. The mask tries to make us feel stupid for changing our minds. As if changing means that we are flawed for not having picked the "right" way to view things in the first place. To ditch the struggle requires that we be willing to give up being right so that we can begin to be happy.

If you view life as a struggle, then that is what you will get. If you start to believe that there is ease in your life, you'll start to get that instead. Changing your opinion about struggle helps you know that nothing stands in the way of what you want. Unlike Sisyphus, you *can* let go of your stone of struggle. When you do, you'll know what it feels like to be truly free.

Part 4
Living Without
a Mask

CHAPTER 14
Living Authentically

"If one advances confidently in the direction of his dreams, and endeavors to live the life which he has imagined, he will meet with a success unexpected in common hours."
Henry David Thoreau

The point of removing the mask is to live authentically from our real selves, unhampered by what we believe others want us to do or be. The stress and energy used to pretend are gone. When we are ourselves, we are free.

Being ourselves has much more impact on the world than all of the "acting" we do when wearing our masks. The impact is made because we show others that we are not afraid to be who we are, imperfections and all. We exemplify that it is also possible for them to remove their masks and live freely. Living authentically invites others to participate in the fullness of life. We are now beyond the "games of the mask." Now we are able to dance together in the joy of truth.

Living with Awareness

When we are in the middle of a dream, we may not realize that we are dreaming. The events in the dream feel very real. But when we wake up, we know that we were dreaming. If we experienced something scary in the dream, sometimes we will wake ourselves up to end that feeling.

LIVING AUTHENTICALLY

Many people go through their whole _
walking sleep. Their sensations are numbed and
feelings dulled. They feel like the pilot light on their
aliveness has gone out. They trudge through life
barely able to put one foot in front of the other.
Living with awareness is like waking up from the
dreaming state. Awareness allows us to take
advantage of what this life has to offer. We will feel
more connected to the world and excited about our
participation in the process of living. We can then
stand in awe of the perfection and beauty which we
all have played a part in creating.

As we remove the layers of our mask to live from
our truth, we will naturally become more aware.
Awareness cannot be forced. It comes from
releasing the tight grip we have on the illusions
(dreams) we have had about ourselves and others.

Awareness is what gives validation and life to our
truth. No longer will our truth be under the weight
of the "mask's lying contract." Awareness gives our
unique truth permission to shine in the world.

When wearing a mask, we carefully avoid self-
responsibility. **Awareness helps us know that
the only responsibility we really have is to
become more aware of what we are doing
with our lives.**

Acting from wakeful consciousness is all that we
really need to do to feel free of the mask. Once we
experience the freedom of being fully conscious, we
will never be completely content with going back
into a dulled, lifeless sleep.

Beyond Analysis

Analysis can be very helpful when we are in search of our truth. It is a way to understand smaller pieces when the larger perspective is overwhelming. But if we continually analyze without going beyond, we may do intellectual violence to ourselves. We can feel like we are always examining ourselves like a specimen inside a jar. We may feel constantly watched and evaluated. It is difficult to feel safe when we have no respite even from our own scrutiny. Analysis can also keep us in judgment mode rather than just loving ourselves and others.

A step beyond analysis is synthesis. Synthesis is a way of putting the pieces into the whole. With synthesis we are able to integrate the parts of ourselves and others. We can then see the joy, humor, and beauty of the world instead of seeing everything with only our critical eye.

Synthesis allows us to make our own order out of chaos. It allows us to see life as synchronistic patterns instead of disjointed events. Synthesis helps us to understand that there is unity to the universe, even though we are able to glimpse only a small portion of it.

Synthesis helps raise the conscious understanding of ourselves and others to a higher level of being. It gives us a sense of peace because it helps us understand that everything is perfect the way it is. Imperfections and all have a place in our world.

There is a time and place for both aɩ synthesis. True synthesis cannot be accomplished unless we understand our life. We do this by analyzing the pieces. And we cannot feel whole until we can put those pieces back together again in our own way. The trick to living an authentic life is to be adept at doing both analysis and synthesis. We must know when each is called for to bring our external life into alignment with our internal truth.

Dedication to Truth and Integrity

To really honor ourselves and others we must have complete dedication to truth and integrity, whatever that is for each of us. For some of us this will be a challenge because there are so many ways, both big and small, that we have deceived ourselves and others.

We must ask ourselves on a regular basis, "Did I tell the truth in this situation?" "Am I honoring my truth, even if it feels uncomfortable?" "Have I shown integrity in this situation?" If we are absolutely honest with ourselves, the answer is no. We often cop out because it is easier not to face the issue directly. We have an amazing slippery ability to skirt confrontation, but this only perpetuates problems internally and with others.

At some level others know our dishonesty and it will be resented. If dishonesty continues for a long period of time, relationships can deteriorate because at a deep level we know that lying hurts us. Telling the truth and living with integrity, will eventually bring self respect and the respect of others. They will feel that we can be trusted to be honest no matter what.

Responsibility goes along with integrity and telling the truth because there are many ways to say the truth. Some ways can be helpful and loving. Other ways can be hurtful or mean. The key is twofold. First the truth must be told from a place of purity. It should not be an attempt to change anyone else. Your intent should be to give information from your reality, which others can choose to use or not use. Secondly, responsible truth intends to challenge the mask's lies to stretch or change old ideas, but not harm the essence of another person.

Also along with the responsibility will come an increased ability to deflect any shame energy. When the truth or lack of integrity is first brought to conscious awareness, inevitably there will be an attempt to suppress it by the mask. If you are confronting your own truth or integrity, your mask may try to get you to take back the truth by bringing out all of the shaming tapes contained in your internal tape library. It also might give your body physical symptoms. These may tell your body, "If you keep saying this, I'll have to punish you."

If you are living from integrity or saying your truth to others, they may pull out all the stops to get you back into line or to cover over the truth, so they will not have to face their issues of truthfulness or lack of integrity.

If you take back the truth or go again..,. your integrity, you have hurt both yourself and others. You have punished yourself, reinforcing that lying is necessary. You have hurt others, because the challenge they so desperately needed and hoped to get from you was denied them. This perpetuates the illusion that the lie must be truth because, "If I can't count on others to tell me the truth, they are not really supporting me."

Lying takes an enormous amount of energy because the truth naturally wants to be heard and expressed. The more we tell the truth, the easier it gets. Truth validates that we really love ourselves and others. Truthfulness says, "I love you enough to give you the gift of truth. This is your opportunity to shed the lies. It is your choice."

Living an Open Life

Openness allows us to access our essence without barriers. When we are open we are in an expansive state, allowing our perspective to take in new positions, possibilities, and understandings. Openness means that we are flexible to changes around us. We are able to respond to people in fresh ways. We are not afraid to try new experiences.

Being open people means that we are continually growing people. Letting information in which we had not been previously exposed to increases our awareness and broadens our knowledge of the world.

To be open requires less energy than being closed. When we are closed it is like putting chairs and tables against a door to barricade ourselves from forces which we believe could harm us. Openness allows us to stand planted in our truth, while outside forces blow by us like a gentle wind.

Some people confuse openness with having no boundaries. They don't realize the difference between barriers and boundaries. Barriers erect walls between us and the rest of the world. **Boundaries radiate from our essence outward, claiming our natural space in the world.** When we claim our space, there is no way that anyone can intrude. Our openness allows our truth to act as our "force field." It naturally protects us while allowing us to connect to others.

To be open means that we freely accept challenges from ourselves and others. Most people do not want to be challenged, so they urge others to shut down too. Like ostriches with their heads in the sand, they think that if they are not challenged they can pretend that everything is fine the way it is.

But openness allows us to challenge the truth. It helps us to see whether we are really feeling fine or covering over wounds which keep us from wholeness. When we are living from our truth, outside challenges do not rock us. They simply confirm our truth at a deeper level.

Releasing the Need to Defend

If we use our body, emotions, and thoughts to bring pure consciousness into our experience, we no longer feel like we need to defend ourselves. We simply *are*. Being without defenses means that no one can attack us. There is nothing to attack. Defenselessness is the ultimate power. It empowers you to be outside all of the "games of the mask."

Defenselessness denies others an enemy. Without an enemy, others have several choices. They can attempt to find wounds within us which still need defense so they can attach their "enemy energy." Or they can find someone else who will more readily take the "enemy energy." Or they can let down their defenses to match our defenselessness.

Regardless of how others respond to our defenselessness, we are choosing it because it is our natural state, from being in pure consciousness. We are not doing it to get any reaction from anyone outside of ourselves.

Redefining Vulnerability as a Power

One day in meditation the words *"Vulnerability Power"* came to me. The words repeated in my mind until I began to focus on what that meant to me. What I wrote surprised me because I had not heard about vulnerability and power going together.

Other people have been uncomfortable with describing vulnerability as a strength. Vulnerability seems to have a negative connotation for many people. I believe the only reason people feel uncomfortable with being vulnerable is that they feel that they can be hurt by making themselves open to others. But my experience has been that the more I know and heal myself, the more my vulnerability feels like a powerful force. This is because I am not afraid of having my humanness "hang out there" for others to see. When I am vulnerable, I don't have to spend energy protecting or hiding myself. With extra energy available, I am able to connect with others from an authentic place. Because there is no game presenting a facade for their benefit, I am not as threatening to others. They can feel safer about being themselves with me. This is what starts the cycle of healing and understanding between myself and others. As my trust of people grows, so does my love and fun for life. The following is what I wrote in meditation:

"*Vulnerability Power* is the strength of balanced receptive and active energy which is at my very core. The outward form is manifested in thoughts, feelings, and actions in my daily life.

Vulnerability has to do with unveiling my essence for the world to see. To do this I have to trust myself and others around me to create a safe space for the real me to come out, even when I may not know what is about to come out.

True vulnerability requires openness. If I am not open, I am in a protective state which requires defenses to be put up to shield the internal victim from abuse. But when I am open, I can allow my heart to connect to the love around me. I can allow my core to share in the universal knowledge. My mind is capable of grasping truths greater than I alone can know.

True power is my ability to think, feel, and act from *my* truth. It is not abusive of others or manipulative. If these traits are present there is no real power. True power is incapable of hurting others because it is in synchrony with universal laws. It helps me understand the larger perspective, seeing the patterns as they are being created, and the ramifications of potential outcomes.

True power requires taking full responsibility for my thoughts, feelings, and actions, yet seeing that in the grand perspective there is nothing I can do without cooperation from all other forces.

True power flows from a source greater than myself, even when I don't realize that it's coming from outside of me. Power flows through me from my core, out into the universe, and back again. If I believe I am the source of this power, and try to control it, I cut off the natural flow.

So what is *Vulnerability Power*? It is the ability to show my truth to the world while acting in a way which honors myself and others. It requires a balance of inflowing and outflowing energy. This means that giving and receiving must be in balance. Receptivity and outward thrusting must be in balance. Intuition and thought must be in balance. Body, mind, and spirit must be in harmony to help me expand on a higher and higher spiral toward universal wholeness.

It is important, along the path to increased *Vulnerability Power,* for me to be a responder instead of a reactor. Reaction is action directed from outside of me. Response comes from the guidance (inner wisdom) within me. A good way to test whether it is a reaction or response is the feeling in my body. If there is contraction, it is reaction. If there is expansion, it is response.

Vulnerability Power allows me to *know* that there is always choice in how I feel, think, and act. There is no burden of responsibility, only a chance to be an observer of myself. When there is choice, there is ability to make change; anything is possible. So *Vulnerability Power* implies no boundaries. There are infinite possibilities because there are so many choices.

Vulnerability Power necessitates sensitivity to myself and others. Sensitivity to personal boundaries. Sensitivity to feelings. Sensitivity to the precious child in each of us. Sensitivity is within all of me when I connect my essence to the the universal network.

Vulnerability Power leads me to true intimacy (Into-Me-See). I am willing to see myself for who I am and act on what I know is right for me to do and be. I know that others will benefit from my being myself and it gives them safety to be who they are. When others feel safe around me, they are more willing to be intimate with me. *Vulnerability Power* has a unique capability of continually seeking the highest good in myself and others. When I practice *Vulnerability Power* I am able, in my openness, to *allow in the love* but *reflect off negativity* with my loving light. Others then are responsible for dealing with their own negativity. This allows them to learn what they need to do for their highest good.

Vulnerability Power requires risk-taking. Usually the thoughts about the risk are much worse than actually doing it because I am meeting my own resistance. When I surrender to my higher self, then I *know* that I am safe in following my guidance. I am always on the edge of growth, facing the unknown. Taking risk allows my courage to grow. This in turn expands my willingness to go deeper inside, to know myself better and love myself and others more.

Vulnerability Power requires remaining centered, no matter what is going on around me. The centeredness emanates from my core. It is like an internal gyroscope, keeping me upright. There will always be tests to my ability to remain centered. But viewing situations as challenges, rather than difficulties, allows me to meet the tests with calm. I know that I am only given tests that I can handle and am ready for. I embrace the challenges as opportunities to stretch me to a higher level.

Vulnerability Power is androgynous. It is a perfect balance of my most positive internal male and female traits. I discard any genetic and societal programming which does not allow me to live from a place of natural, gentle strength. I am able to connect from my heart while acting from my truth. I am able to allow my intuition and intellect to act in harmony. And, I am able to speak my truth while honoring other people's feelings.

My vision of *Vulnerability Power* for the world becomes clearer as I strip away my falsity to get down to my own naked truth. I am no longer afraid of nurturing other's *Vulnerability Power*. I value differences between myself and others. I stand in awe of other's unique beauty. I know that no one else can be who I am, so I am not threatened by others showing me who they are. I see that we each have a special part in the world, like threads in an elaborate tapestry.

We can each be pioneers in *Vulnerability Power* at any time we choose. It requires experimenting with different ways of being. That is part of the fun of life, finding greater ways to love ourselves and others. Leaping into the unknown also expands the possibilities for generations to come. Let us each remember that at the point we trust enough to leap, it will become clear where we are to land."

Living Simply

Simplicity is stripping away all that is inessential. It is living an uncluttered life. Simplicity allows our essence to appear in the world without needing to compete for attention or defend our actions.

Our essence is simple. What we put over it to keep it down is complex and unneeded. Truth is simple. The lies we manufacture to cover truth are complex. So living simply relieves us of the burden of complexity. We are untangling the chains which have put a stranglehold on our lives.

Living simply is not living poorly. Poverty implies there is no choice. There are people who are considered "financially poor" by others' standards. But these people derive richness from their internal lives. They are filled with joy and love for life. They see things as unnecessary to their happiness. They do not consider themselves poor.

There can be financially rich people, who live in "internal" poverty. They are encumbered with outside complication which keeps them from living freely. They feel they have no choice but to keep doing what makes them financially secure.

Living simply does not mean that we must live without things which give us comfort. It does mean that things must serve us, rather than our serving them. If we stay in a house we dislike because we feel that some day it will bring us a profit, we are serving our things. We let things serve us if we live in a house which comforts us and feels like a haven.

Stripping away what is unnecessary to get to the simplicity is a process as well as a goal. When we live with awareness, we must ask ourselves every day if we are living simply. Are we living in a way which encourages our truth to come out? Are we encouraging ourselves to live free of the clutter which drains so much of most people's energy? Are we allowing our true needs and desires to be fulfilled? When we can answer yes to all of these questions, we experience the freedom which simplicity brings into our lives.

Living Free

Freedom has been discussed a lot in this book. Freedom to show our truth to the world. Freedom to express ourselves. Freedom from the oppression of others.

We have seen repeatedly that self-examination and independent thinking are keys to living freely. When we know ourselves, we are not afraid of being challenged. This does not mean we are gullible. We are able to stay open to input from others without feeling we must take on their understanding of the world as our own.

Wearing masks has shackled us. Living freely means we release ourselves from our self-imposed bondage. It is a lifelong process of looking more deeply within ourselves to see where we are still chained and choosing to let go.

Being free means that we are able to release what passes through our lives. This is whether loved ones die, relationships become outdated, we move to a different place, we change jobs, or situations hurt us. Freedom is letting go so we can accept the new.

Staying with Ourselves So We Can be with Others

Great teachers through the ages have constantly said that we must be truly with ourselves if we want to be with others. For years I thought I was doing that until I realized a very important thing about myself.

In a meditation the image came to me that when I was with others, my energy left my space and jumped across to be in the other person's space. As my energy "arced across" to be with the other, I left myself. It was as if all that was left of me was a deadened shell. Consequently, my connection with others did not have the vitality I wanted it to have.

I now understand that I must never leave my space to be with anyone else. I practice awareness to stay centered within my body and radiate my energy outward. When I do this, my *essence* connects to others in a way that was not possible when I leave myself. My centeredness affirms the fact that I do not need to sacrifice myself to get the connections with others that I want. It affirms to others that they are important enough to me to touch them with my essence.

"Taking Off the Brake" to Live Life Fully

An image came to mind one day. I felt like I was going through life too fast with the brakes on. I felt like I was moving faster than my natural pace, and at the same time, I was moving against extra unnecessary force. In concentrating on this image, I realized that if I felt like I had a brake on my *outflowing* energy, the same must be true for my *inflowing* energy. I saw that this internal image was blocking my ability to act from my full capacity of strength.

I began to alter my perception of having the brake on by focusing on an image of myself without the brakes. At first in the image I was hurtling downhill unchecked, afraid that I would careen over a cliff.

I decided to change the image so that I was instead on a roller coaster. (I have always had fun on roller coasters because I know that even though I have a sense of being out of control, I really am safe.) In the image the roller coaster climbs to heights, plunges to depths, takes in unknown twists and turns, but eventually ends up safely on level ground.

The roller coaster image has become my symbol for trusting to go forward in life without the brakes on. The track represents my mission in life, guided by a source greater than myself. The dips and turns represent the unknown ahead of me. These are the challenges I must meet. The rush of the ride comes in the abandon with which I face the track ahead, in spite of my fears. Letting go of my brakes (the illusion that I am in control) allows me to have carefree fun with whatever happens. When I am able to hold this image of life, I know that I am flowing freely, totally safe on my own track.

Living with Bliss

Living with bliss may take some getting used to. After all, not many of us have had role models for how to live authentically while radiating bliss. Maybe this is why the few people who seem to be truly blissful are idealized. But we can *all* experience the same feelings within. We just have to "stretch our bliss muscles."

At first, when bliss starts coming to us, we may feel like it is a fluke. We have been conditioned to believe that something bad must follow, if something good happens. We may hold our breath "waiting for the other shoe to drop" or feel there is disappointment waiting for us right around the corner. If that is the way we think, we probably will have that experience.

Bliss can begin to permeate our feelings even when challenging situations arise. We will start to believe, and then finally know, that *bliss is a state of mind available at all times.*

Bliss also does not require us to be continually happy, or "up" all of the time. Bliss runs deeper than these temporary surface feelings. There will be times when we are in pain or dealing with difficulty that is not pleasurable. True bliss can be experienced even during these times, because every experience we have allows us to be fully alive, growing human beings.

You may want to try this test periodically to see how blissful you really are. In the middle of a challenging situation ask yourself, "Am I feeling bliss now even though I don't like what's happening?" When you can truly answer yes, you will know that you are finally letting your natural bliss state surface and spill over into your outside life.

Living in the Gap

What is the Gap? The gap is the space between. The silence. The process. It is what makes us human *beings* instead of human *doings*. The gap is the place where we connect to ourselves and others. It is like the silence between notes in the music.

We live in the gap by listening in silence, observing, and being still. Living in the gap allows our receptivity to flourish. We become the excited student again, eager to learn what life has to offer.

Hearing the messages of silence

Listening to the silence opens a completely new dimension of communication. Through the silence we can tap into the collective knowledge of the universe around us. The silence can "speak" to us in pictures, thoughts, vibrations, colors, or voices. The speech of silence comes from beyond the five senses. At this level of awareness, there is a whole new, exciting world to explore.

A new language of nature may come forward in the silence. We can hear the soothing lullabies of the high country stream, the powerful strength in the force of the wind, and the wisdom of the ages in the graceful cedar tree.

The silence helps us feel "glued together." There is sense of connection which helps us feel the sacredness in everything around us. Silence anchors us to our core because it shows our essence we are open to listening to our inner desires and deep personal knowledge.

Silence helps us to see life from a higher perspective. We can suspend our need to judge situations and let ourselves look at things with new eyes. As we open to new possibilities, our old crustiness starts to fall away. In place of the old crustiness always come new ways of opening our hearts.

When we are busy, talking all of the time, or thinking about the past or future, it is difficult for the messages of silence to come through. But when we quiet our minds, the messages can emerge with great clarity. The messages are usually simple and to the point. The message may be,"Be still," "Feel," "Breathe," "Open your heart," "Support is all around you," "Connect to the love already here." When we

LIVING WITHOUT A MASK

let go of the noise around and within us, the messages from the silence penetrate to our core. They help us to feel comfort and safety, knowing that our truth is our best guide through life.

Quieting the turbulent mind

If we are not used to listening to the silence, it can be very difficult to get our "chatterbox" mind to be quiet. The "chatterbox" mind is a turbulent mind, never giving us respite from the hubbub around us.

There is a reason that our mind feels compelled to keep talking. It has been taught by the mask that there must be constant movement. The turbulent mind is kept anxious and fearful because it is in this state that we are most likely to buy into the mask's lies.

The mask knows, as does our essence, that when the mind is quiet, our pure consciousness will emerge. That is the ultimate threat to the mask. If we are in a state of pure consciousness, we do not need a mask. We are beyond it. The mask is impotent against the powerful force of pure consciousness.

What we must do is practice *going beyond thinking* to invite the mind to stop talking. Meditation is one of the most useful ways of accessing the quiet mind. There are other ways that may work for you to quiet your turbulent mind.

Whatever method you use, once you have experienced the silence, you will want to go back to it over and over. Never again will you be able to completely tolerate the constant chatter of the turbulent mind.

Balancing

If all of these pieces about owning our truth and living authentically seem like an incredible balancing act, you are right. Some of the areas in our lives which need to be balanced for us to live our truth are:

1. Work and play
2. Activity and quiet time
3. Wakefulness and sleeping
4. Feeling and thinking
5. Connection with others and solitude
6. Acting like adults and acting like children
7. Giving and receiving
8. Expressing and listening
9. Doing and being
10. Filling up and emptying out
11. Holding on and letting go
12. Seriousness and humor

In Dr. Seuss' book *Oh, the Places You'll Go!* he says it so well:

> "You'll get mixed up, of course,
> As you already know.
> You'll get mixed up
> With many strange birds as you go.

LIVING WITHOUT A MASK

So be sure when you step.
Step with care and great tact
and remember that Life's a Great Balancing Act.
Just never forget to be dexterous and deft.
And *never* mix up you right foot with your left."*

* Dr. Seuss, *Oh the Places You'll Go!* (New York: Random House, 1990).

CHAPTER 15
A World Free From Masks

"When we change our way of seeing,
we begin to live in a different world."
Eknath Easwaran

Envisioning a world without masks is not a utopian fantasy. It is something achievable now, without any other resources than what we already have. *We* are the resource, individually and collectively.

Teaching Our Children Not to Wear Masks

All of the effort we must expend on ourselves to remove the mask does not need to be done over again by our children. We can teach them how to live without masks, to live life more fully.

Most parents now see their job as disciplining their children to help them cope in the world. If instead we saw the role of parent as teaching children how to *parent themselves*, children would not have as much need to wear masks. They would not be afraid of asserting their individuality and speaking their truth.

The same thing applies in our educational system. The whole idea of an "educational system" is inherently flawed to begin with. We believe that giving children information (or education) is helping them to live in the world. It is not education that children need. It is knowledge, not facts, figures, or theory. We must begin to shift our educational perception from stuffing children with rote "learned" material, to assisting them in *acquiring their own knowledge*. The role of teachers would then change from that of authority figures to role models through teaching children to teach themselves.

Teaching our children to teach themselves is the key in other areas of their lives, such as spirituality. Rather than setting down religious rules and dogma which are like grooves that we expect our children to fit into, we can best serve our children when we understand that they have a completely perfect spiritual connection of their own. Nurturing children's unique spiritual connection is the role of real spiritual leaders. Teaching children that they *can find all of their own answers* by listening to their inner truth should be a global goal.

In the area of health, we must also teach our children from the model that perfect health is available to all. It is available to anyone who wants to tap into it. We can help children from the time they are babies to listen to their bodies' physical needs. They can understand how to use their emotions to find out what their truth is telling them, and learn the ability to take action when it is called for. Once again we assist children best when we teach them how to *listen to their own (not our) internal truth about health.*

All aspects of children's lives are drastically altered when we see them as human beings equal with adults. They are complete with perfect essences and their own truth. Their truths and essences only need to be nurtured to grow, flourish, and gain experience. Then instead of spending time to remove limiting masks, they can spend energy exploring who they are and expressing that creatively in the world.

Redefining Leadership

Leaders, whether they be presidents and prime ministers of countries or presidents of P.T.A.'s, are no different internally than the rest of us. Many of the leaders, however, have fearful, out of control children within which motivate them. In their fear, they lash out by attempting to control others. They believe that if enough other people are made to do their bidding, it will make them more powerful.

Some leaders want to be liked, so don't really take a leadership role. Their positions on issues change as the opinion polls change. Their validation still comes from the outside because they don't feel good about their own inner wisdom.

There are a few real leaders. These are men and women who are willing to see themselves and others clearly because they know and love themselves. Some of the qualities of true leaders are:

Real leaders guide from their inner wisdom.
They truly lead by trusting their own truth and knowledge. They are not swayed by popularity because they do not need outside confirmation of their internal truth. Their leadership emanates from within and spreads outward without being forced.

Real leaders are facilitators.
Their strength comes from honoring other human beings and the faith that human nature has the ability to achieve its best. They know that their role is to support the unfolding of the individual and their collective highest purpose. Real leaders teach people how to *lead themselves*.

Real leaders are responsive to world changes.
They are able to be responsive rather than reactive to new information and situations. They welcome change because it means that the process of their leadership is still flowing. They do not need to cling to power or position. They know that their leadership comes from their ability to adapt to the needs and growth of those they lead.

Real leaders see the global implications of their actions.
They are cognizant that they must look at every potential choice for how it will affect others. They desire to contribute to the local, national, and world's highest purpose. They are willing to let go of their leadership position, if necessary, to accomplish this highest purpose.

Real leaders know integrity starts with them.
They know that they cannot expect an organization or society which they lead to operate with integrity if they do not fully embrace their own integrity. This means that they may have to make unpopular decisions and shake up the status quo to ensure that the commitment to truth is carried through.

Real leaders are gentle.
They have no need to fulfill some outdated "macho" stereotype just to placate narrow expectations. They realize that all people, even those under a tough exterior, need gentle nurturing. They understand how to give that to others even while being firm in not accepting anyone's attempts at bullying behavior.

Real leaders are empathetic.
They know that hardness does not show real strength. Therefore, they are not afraid to show their soft caring side to others. This also applies to their negotiations. Real leaders know that they demonstrate leadership when they display caring about all positions presented.

Real leaders are open to new ways to develop mutual trust.
Whether real leaders are dealing with people on a one-on-one basis or they are working with large groups of people, they remain open to creative ways of communicating which will foster mutual trust

between all parties. They are willing to listen to others' ideas of how to bring everyone closer. And they are willing to drop outmoded ways which no longer fit.

Real leaders know that the best way of developing mutual trust is to disarm themselves. They are willing to be the first to show others they are not afraid of what the trust will bring.

Leading the Leaders

To develop the kind of leaders who will guide us collectively into a world free from masks requires that we "lead our leaders into leadership." Some points about leading our leaders are:

The collective will of the people is always ultimately more powerful than any tyranny.

When we live from our individual strength, no one can make us collectively do what we are not willing to do.

When we act from strength, leaders have no choice but to reach inside themselves to find their own strength.

Weak leaders' and tyrants' survival at the top depends on weakness in those they lead. They cannot stay in power if those being led demand excellence and real leadership.

A WORLD FREE FROM MASKS

When individuals no longer tolerate fighting and wars as a solution to conflict, leaders will stop proposing fighting as a problem-solving tool.
There is a well-known saying, "Fighting is what you do when you aren't willing to look at options." Broadening our perspective to see common ground rather than fighting helps us find solutions to conflict. What better form of world disarmament can there be than for all of us to lay down our facades and radiate that we are not afraid of who we or others really are.

We can lead our leaders by living our own lives in the direction we want the planet to go. This means that all of the traits of leadership which we want in others, we must draw out in ourselves. In his book, *Gifts From Eykis*, Wayne Dyer speaks of human beings' five "fuzzy" thinking categories:

> Quality instead of Appearance thinking
> Ethics instead of Rules thinking
> Knowledge instead of Achievement thinking
> Integrity instead of Domination thinking
> Serenity instead of Acquisition thinking*

Clarifying our thinking so we live from quality, ethics, knowledge, integrity, and serenity, means that we naturally lead. We, individually, do not need to

---

* Wayne Dyer, *Gifts From Eykis* (New York: Pocket Books, 1983), p. 128–129.

be recognized by the public to be leaders. **Our example is what leads, not words.**

Uniting Our Truths for a World Without Masks

When we talk about uniting our truths to live in a world without masks, we do not have to give up our truth, or individuality, to adopt one world truth. An unmasked world will be lived through people who *give of* their individuality to further change, not *give up* their individuality for change. Sacrificing ourselves would defeat the purpose. And it would not accomplish a world without masks. Self-sacrifice only shows that we are still hiding behind the mask of a martyr.

There is a community activists saying, "From diversity comes our strength." Uniting our truth means that we each focus our individual truth toward the idea of betterment of the whole. As we live our truth, the whole world becomes stronger.

We have no idea what the whole story is for this beloved planet. We provide our talents, insight, love, and caring and then trust that the rest will be taken care of in a pattern greater than we each can fully understand.

Playing the Game
of Life Without Masks

Much of what we have done in this book is examine how we play the game of life from behind a mask. We have explored ways to stop playing these games. We have seen how the "games of the mask" extract a high price from us and the entire planet. Only we can decide if we are willing to continue to sacrifice ourselves for the sake of the games. Or are we willing to do what it takes to be totally free.

The childlike part of us loves to play games. If there is no game around, we will find something to make into a game. We are afraid that life will become dull and serious without the games that we have become familiar with.

But living without a mask is anything but dull. No longer do we need to hide behind bullying, victimization, manipulation, gullibility, fear, and struggle. Without our masks, those things dissolve to reveal our real selves.

Our creativity at discovering new ways of living flourishes. Now we can live with the childlike joy which is our birthright. We can develop new games to play which allow others to play with us in our new found freedom. We may be surprised to find how many people are really tired of the old games and were just waiting for ways to experiment with living life differently. Some possible features for our new games might be:

LIVING WITHOUT A MASK

Players see attempts at manipulation by others as others' problems.
In the new game of life, players do not take on the negative energy of anyone who tries to manipulate. It is made clear to those who manipulate that their behavior is "understandable, but not acceptable." Players become more and more skilled at dealing with the real person under the manipulative mask, bypassing the surface interference which is thrown out by the mask caricature.

Players speak their truth.
Even at the expense of short-term alienation, everyone must act from their truth. There is no desire to pacify another with a "white lie" or a compliment which is not sincere. Players learn that speaking their truth ultimately draws others, who are also truthful, to them. As players discover more of their truth, they are willing to share this new perspective with others. The goal and the process is increased internal clarity and understanding between the players.

Players learn to respond to others.
When challenging situations arise, players reach inside of themselves for how to deal with others, staying true to their integrity and inner guidance. What others think of them does not influence the players' decisions.

Players are not responsible for any other adult but themselves.
There is freedom and lightness in no longer being responsible for actions, feelings, or outcome of other people's lives. This is not to say that players will not care about others. They will still do whatever their truth and integrity guides them to do for others. Players display their caring for people, but they know that others must choose their own perceptions and actions.

Players develop the ability to go with the flow.
When circumstances change, players are able to adapt. They no longer cling to rigid ideas which no longer fit the new situations. They are like the willow which bends gracefully in the wind rather than the brittle stick which gets easily broken.

Players develop the ability to laugh at themselves.
Players are not afraid to be themselves, even when they appear foolish. Being willing to look silly, strange, weird, or ridiculous before others is considered a sign of maturity. It can also be fun. When players are not afraid to appear foolish, no one can manipulate them by threatening to make them look ridiculous. They have already done that for themselves.

Players sing, dance, laugh, connect with nature, and enjoy themselves every day.

The "life force" dosage requirement may vary from player to player. There can be "life force meter stations" (similar to blood pressure check stations at some drug stores) which the players can plug into any time they want to check to see if their daily dosage of enjoyment is being met.

CHAPTER 16
Letting Go to Receive the New

"Freedom—Letting come what comes. Letting go what goes."
Deepak Chopra

When I used to think of letting go, I thought of myself as holding onto the edge of a rocky, steep cliff. Below me, I could see only sharp rocks which I believed would impale me if I let go of my grip. My knuckles turned white and my muscles ached, but still I clung to the rocks, afraid of what would happen to me if I let go.

But my inner voice kept getting stronger, saying, "Let go. Let go." My body cried out to let go. And my heart pounded and acknowledged that it was time to let go.

When I finally decided I had to do it and risk what I felt was sure death, my image changed. At the instant I let go, I looked below me. Instead of seeing sharp rocks, I saw a pile of big fluffy pillows lying in a grassy field.

Then I knew that the image I had carried for so long was only one which my mask was using to keep me from letting go. The mask was trying to keep me from relaxing and experiencing peace, happiness, and joy.

There are still times when my inner voice tells me to let go and I am afraid to do so. When I remember my original experience, it is easier to let go. I realize now that my holding on to any issue or person is only an illusion resulting from my past conditioning. All that letting go really means is releasing the old, to accept the newness that life has to offer.

Embracing the Unknown

Removing the mask, as we have seen over and over, is a process of releasing what we have been clinging to and hiding behind. It requires that we attune to our own truth and the desires of our very essence.

To do this, we must first rid ourselves of old outdated feelings, beliefs, and understandings. They have been ours for a long time, but they no longer serve us. Releasing allows us to have room within to accept the new.

In the process of letting go, there will be times when we will need to feel empty. Emptiness precedes expansion. It is the period of gestation before the birth of the new. Simply allowing ourselves to feel the emptiness without impeding it is called for, if we want to accept the new. We have planted the seeds of acceptance by simply opening. Now we must wait for the gifts of the unknown to come to us and be ready to receive them when they arrive.

The Process of Removing the Mask, Summary

No matter what the specific change process we go through to remove our mask, there are helpful reminders which can apply in almost any situation. There is no order to these points and the list is not comprehensive. It is intended only to be a basis for you to design your own unique list. Remember, you define your own process as you go. Allow yourself time to evolve into the person you want to be. Let go into the process of *BEING YOU!*

Your Perception

- You are responsible for your feelings, thoughts, and perceptions.
- Your feelings, thoughts, and perceptions hold clues to your truth.
- Know that you *always* have choices.
- No one can make you feel or believe anything you do not want to feel or believe.
- Take pieces of what others tell you which fit for you. Throw out the rest.
- Trust your reality over others'.
- See "problems and difficulties" as "lessons, opportunities, and gifts."

Observe Yourself
- Be your own nonjudgmental observer.
- Be willing to step back and see the "bigger picture" and patterns in your life.
- Trust your body to give you important signs about your truth.
- Be willing to examine yourself over and over to access more of your truth.

Observe Others
- Separate people's behavior from their essence.
- Be willing to see others' behavior as a caricature of the real person.
- Others are making life up as they go. No one has "the answer."
- Don't take others too seriously.
- See yourself as a peer with everyone else.

Your Emotions
- Allow your emotions to guide you to your truth.
- Be willing to feel your pain fully, so it can be released.
- Release fearing others and they no longer have power over you.
- Listen to the underlying message of your anger, so the energy can be directed toward the change you really want.

How You Act
- Become a responder instead of a reactor.
- Honor the boundaries of yourself and others.
- Allow yourself to be imperfect and make mistakes.
- Don't let yourself be rushed into decisions.
- It's okay to change your mind.
- Be guided by your intuition before your intellect.
- Be willing to stand alone in your truth and you'll never be lonely.

Nurture Yourself
- Allow yourself time to change.
- Change is not a smooth progression. Know that you may have to go back to old ways to learn they no longer serve you.
- Be willing to listen and act on your inner desires.
- Balance your desires for play and work.
- Allow yourself to laugh, sing, dance and enjoy living.
- Be gentle with yourself.
- **Love yourself unconditionally. This means mask and all!**

Index

Index

Index

Index

About the Author

Marion Moss has a B.S. in Communications from the University of Texas. She was a consumer fraud investigator for the Texas Attorney General's Office for 8 years. During this time, she developed an understanding of how individuals are manipulated and their fears used against them. She was an investigative training coordinator and has written training manuals and taught on this subject at the local and national level.

During the last 12 years Marion has also been on an internal journey, exploring her relationship to herself and others. She continues to heal and nurture her inner wounds while expanding and discovering her strengths. "Negative" past experiences are reframed into "learning steps" on her individual path.

Marion currently lives in Seattle. In addition to writing, she teaches classes and facilitates workshops which focus on transforming participants' individual "weaknesses" into strengths.

Classes and Workshops

Some of the topics Marion Moss currently teaches are:

•**Profile of the Con Artist**™
See con artists for the scared children they really are and learn how to end being "hooked" by them.

•**Turning Gullibility into Wisdom**™
Understand adult bullies' mentality and methods they use to exploit weaknesses of others.

•**Dealing with Workplace Bullies**™
Stop victimization by bosses, co-workers, customers, and others.

•**Maintaining Your Integrity at Work**™
Learn how you can stay true to your ideals and ethics in real life work situations.

•**Trading Fear for Freedom**™
Listen to the real messages of fear, to redirect "fear energy" into constructive areas of your life.

•**Develop Your "Courage Power Pack"**™
You can realize your full potential in spite of your fears.

•**Ditching the Struggle**™
Say goodbye to struggle and hello to life's excitement.

•**Redefining Vulnerability as Power**™
Connect from your heart while acting from *your* truth.

•**Escaping the Mind Game Trap**™
End mentally "chasing your tail." Use your mind to create freedom and bliss for yourself.

For information about presentations, Marion can be contacted at (206) 633-5742.

Order Form
for additional books:

Removing Your Mask
No More Hiding From Your Truth

Book	Price	Qty.	Amount
Removing Mask	$13.95	_____	_____

Shipping & Handling: Add $2.00
  for 1st book, 50¢ for each additional   _____

Washington residents add 8.2% sales tax
  (for 1 book sales tax is $1.14)   _____
                                      Total   _____

Enclose order with check or money order and mail to:
Orion Publishing Company
539 Queen Anne Ave. N., Suite 156
Seattle, WA   98109

<u>Send this order to</u>:
Name: _____

Address: _____

City: _____ State: _____ Zip: _____

Phone in case we need to call you regarding your order:

Home: (____)_____ Work: (___)_____

Please allow 3-4 weeks for delivery.